VICTOR

The True Story of My Journey
Through Tragedy, Addiction, and Recovery

BOB ANDERSON

PALMETTO
PUBLISHING
Charleston, SC
www.PalmettoPublishing.com

Copyright © 2024 by Bob Anderson

Cover Art by: Joshua Hay
Technical Advisor: Derek Smith
Transcribed by: Jenny Anderson

Paperback ISBN: 979-8-8229-4168-7

Victim or **Victor**—the choice is yours.

Victor—*A person who defeats an enemy or opponent in a battle, game, or other competition.*

CONTENTS

INTRODUCTION

As I look back on my life, I'm amazed how it all unfolded.
Several of my friends have told me that I should
write the story of my life. I've been meaning to do this for years,
but I'm finally putting pen to paper. From 12-12–56
when I was born to the present day, my story spans 62 years and
continues to amaze me to this day.

I've included all documentation of certain events.
This is the true story of my life.
Unbelievable but true.
I've left people's last names out for their own
confidentiality and privacy.

The story of my life has a lot of negative events and tragedies.
I've tried to also include as many positive events as I can.
I know the reader might get tired of all the tragedies,
car accidents, etc., but there is light at the end of the tunnel.

CHAPTER 1

THE BEGINNING

On December 12, 1956, at Latter Day Saints Hospital in Salt Lake City at 4:37 PM, I was born into this world. My father, George Robert Anderson, was 33, and my mother Nancy Lou Anderson was 22. They lived at 1372 Glen Rose Dr. in Salt Lake City. At the time, the government was experimenting with nuclear explosives at the Nevada test site. There were more than 100 above ground nuclear warhead explosions that filled the sky with bright orange fireballs that dissolved into purplish mushroom clouds. 27 of the later explosions were more powerful than the bomb that dropped on Hiroshima. The atomic energy commission waited until the winds were "favorable "before conducting its tests.

Favorable meant blowing east away from the heavily populated city of Las Vegas and Los Angeles, but directly at such sparsely populated areas as St. George and Salt Lake City, Utah. As a result, before the nuclear test ban treaty was signed in 1963, and for years afterward, the impact of the atomic weapons testing on innocent citizens was devastating. Their results were cancer leukemia, Hodgkin's disease, birth defects, and mental retardation, and other health issues.

During the mid-set of the 1955 testing program, John Wayne spent 30 days on a Saint George location, filming his role as Genghis Khan in "the conqueror". Wayne later died of cancer. So did his costar, Susan Hayward, the Director, Dick Powell, and 10 of the extras.

In the spring of 1953, more than 4000 sheep died suddenly. Many lambs were born with defects. Two ranchers sued the government but lost. A federal judge later ruled that the government covered up evidence in a 1956 lawsuit. The cattle were also affected by radioactive fallout. They had radioactive milk, which went into Las Vegas for processing and distribution.

MURDER BY GOVERNMENT
Nuclear Deaths in a Small Town
Report by Michele Willens

At the start of the second half of the 20th century it would have been hard to find a more typical American small town than St. George, Utah. Located midway between Las Vegas and Salt Lake City on Interstate 15, its 4,500 residents were deeply religious and patriotic people. They were proud of their impressive Mormon Tabernacle, the clean air and the healthy climate. They could sit on their front porches at night, listening to the crickets hum and watching the sun set over the Indian-red mountains in the distance. Still, they showed more than passing concern for events happening outside of Washington County, such as the continuing conflict in Korea and the escalating Cold War tensions between the United States and the Soviet Union.

And then something began happening—145 miles away in the Nevada desert—that would radically alter most of their lives. The first of more than 100 aboveground nuclear-warhead explosions at the Nevada Test Site filled the sky with bright-orange fireballs that dissolved into purplish mushroom clouds. Twenty-seven of the later explosions were more powerful than the bomb dropped on Hiroshima.

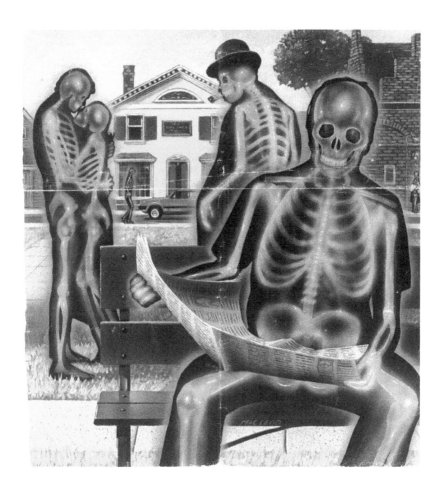

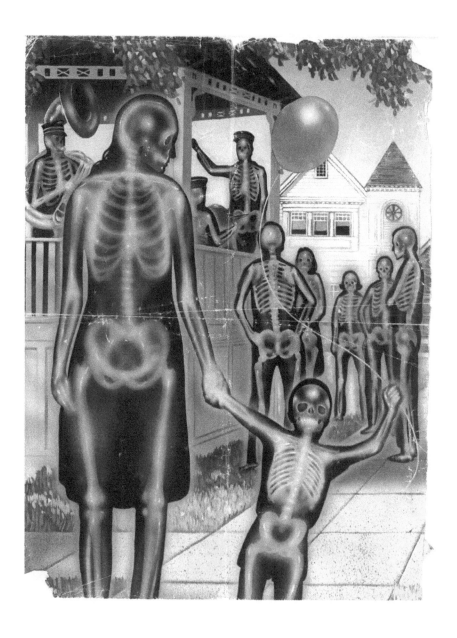

"You are in a very real sense active participants in the nation's atomic-test program," the Atomic Energy Commission informed the citizens of St. George early in 1955. "You have been close observers of tests which have contributed greatly to building the defenses of our own country and of the free world. ... You have accepted the inconvenience or the risk without fuss, without alarm and without panic."

Unquestioning townspeople felt secure even when the ground beneath them trembled on the days the devices were detonated. They paid scant attention to the gray ash that filtered from their skies, covered the neighboring farmlands and soiled freshly laundered clothes that were hanging out to dry.

"They always told us there was no danger, nothing to worry about," says one resident. "Even on the occasions when the AEC people told us to stay indoors for a few hours, they always assured us everything would be all right."

Those assurances continued even when, on afternoons following particularly heavy blasts, some inhabitants began feeling like their skin had been badly sunburned. They continued even after all cars coming through St. George were stopped by local and state police, who directed them to a service station for radiation detection. "The cars were so hot with radiation that the geiger counters went nuts," recalls one station operator.

The trouble was that fallout from the mushroom clouds forming over the desert invariably took flight on the wind. The AEC waited until winds were "favorable" before conducting its tests. Favorable meant blowing east, away from the heavily populated cities of Las Vegas and Los Angeles but directly at such sparsely populated areas as St. George. As a result—before the Nuclear Test Ban Treaty was signed in 1963 and for years afterward—the impact of atomic-weapons testing on innocent citizens was devastating.

One woman, Mrs. Irma Thomas, stands as a stunning example. She lives off dusty St. George Boulevard in a modest stucco home enclosed by a white picket fence. She takes down a photograph of her pretty, longhaired daughter from a bookshelf to show a visitor. The girl had been a dancer before being incapacitated by a severe muscle disease. Two of her other daughters have had operations for precancerous growths. Another has had three miscarriages. Mrs. Thomas's sister and sister-in-law both died of cancer. Her husband presently suffers from skin cancer. And her brother has been in and out of a Salt Lake City hospital for treatment of what most probably is cancer.

The elderly woman walks slowly to her front window. "The doctor's wife died in that house," she says, pointing across the street. "The next one down is where the former sheriff died of bone cancer. One house over, another friend recently died of leukemia. I don't think there's a house on the block where someone hasn't had some form of cancer."

Three blocks away, on Tabernacle Street, the St. George Cemetery is jampacked with tombstones hardly more than a foot apart. A recent surplus of bodies has prompted the addition of a substantial new burial section across the street. "In the time we've been here, the big majority of deaths have been from cancer," confirms Rick Metcalf of the Metcalf Mortuary. "An alarming number of them have happened in the last ten years or so. I just buried Mary Leisek. She died of breast cancer. And we have a funeral service tomorrow for a Mr. Todd. Cancer got him too."

But at long last many of those who reside in this town of the living dead are fighting back. More than 1,000 people from St. George and the surrounding region have filed a multimillion-dollar lawsuit against the federal government, claiming that they or their relatives suffered or died from some form of cancer caused by radiation exposure resulting from the nuclear testing. They are asking the courts for compensation to meet their heavy medical needs, to hold those responsible accountable and to prevent such incidents from occurring in the future.

The issue at hand is simply this: Even though there is no definitive way to link an individual's cancer with exposure to radiation experienced years earlier, how can the government continue to ignore the alarming number of victims?

"Let's put it this way," says St. George lawyer McArthur Wright. "How many people have you known in your lifetime who died of leukemia—cancer of the blood? Well, everyone around here knows at least five or six."

A study by Dr. Joseph L. Lyon, an assistant professor at the University of Utah College of Medicine, supplies increasing evidence of the harmful effects of radiation from nuclear-weapons testing. It shows that children born near the Nevada Test Site during the period when 84 aboveground explosions occurred had two-and-one-half times the leukemia-death rate of children born either before the test program began or after it had ended.

"Before and after the testing we never had more than maybe one or two mentally retarded children," adds Dr. Sheldon Johnson, a St. George optometrist for 28 years who served on the town's school board for 21 years. "But around 1958 we suddenly had about 16 deformed and retarded children and had to form a special classroom unit just for them. I don't think there's been one case since the testing ended in 1963."

Today St. George offers a curious mixture of doom and boom. A controlled-growth plan has increased the population to 10,000. New shopping malls, four golf courses and at least 24 real-estate offices reflect the expanding community that has been touted as one of the nation's ideal places for retirement. But there also exists a nagging insecurity traceable to the premature demise of so many longtime residents.

"Anytime someone aches in this town, we get nervous," says Maxine Smith, a local office worker.

"I'm sure that when I go, it will be cancer," adds a former resident. "And that's pretty much the sentiment of all of us who grew up in St. George."

A frequently heard example of gallows humor underscores the town's uneasy mood. "What do young people do on a Saturday night in St. George?" someone asks. The response: "They die."

Another joke compares St. George and Las Vegas, just two hours away by car. "Vegas is where you go to play Keno, but this is where you stay and have Chemo," says one local, referring to chemotherapy treatment for cancer.

Yet it's hard to imagine a friendlier, more trusting group of people than those who reside here. Only recently, hardware-store owner Elmer Pickett greeted a customer who came in to pay him for items purchased weeks before.

"Haven't you been waiting for this?" the man asked, handing Pickett a check.

"Forgot all about it, but I'll never turn it down," the storekeeper grinned.

A baldish fellow nearing 60 years of age, Pickett is one of those suing the government. He has good cause: Ten of his relatives have died of cancer.

"I think we were had, and those who lied should be held responsible," he says. "I'm not in this for the money. I could never make back what it cost me to try to save my wife's life."

Viola Pickett and her mother both died of cancer. Viola was tending her garden on May 19, 1953, when the Atomic Energy Commission exploded a nuclear device placed atop a 300-foot iron tower near Yucca Flats inside the Nevada Test Site. The resulting cloud—full of radioactive dirt, particles from the tower and other debris—came to be called Dirty Harry. The blast immediately dumped 6,000 millirems of radiation on St. George. (The AEC limit at the time was 3,900 millirems per 13-week period; today the accepted standard is 500 millirems annually.)

"It was so dirty that radio bulletins told us to go inside until further notice," Elmer Pickett recalls. "But being outside, Viola never heard the radio and got well-dosed with fallout. She wasn't yet 40 when she died, and I was left with six kids, the youngest two-and-a-half. I felt the emotional damage of her loss long after she died."

Building inspector Scott Prisbrey has lived in St. George most of his life. The ruddy-faced man can hardly hold back the tears when he talks of watching his son die. Chad Prisbrey was just a youngster early in 1953 when he and the other children used to run outside at dawn to watch the clouds of nuclear dust coming over the horizon.

"He was a healthy young man," says Prisbrey. "But in the spring of his 27th year he suddenly started having problems. He was sleeping all the time, getting nosebleeds and losing feeling in his hands. We were constantly taking him to the hospital in Salt Lake City. I've never seen anyone go through such torture. By November he was dead of Hodgkin's disease."

Hodgkin's disease is a terminal condition characterized by progressive enlargement of the lymph glands, spleen and liver, as well as progressive anemia. "We didn't even know what Hodgkin's *was* before the testing," notes a former St. George mortician.

"You can understand a child dying in an automobile accident maybe, or a war, but to die from radiation and have no say is criminal," Prisbrey continues. "If the AEC people had told us the truth at the time—that there might be some health hazards later on—we'd have moved away before testing began. I'm part of the lawsuit because it may prevent things like this from happening again. But all the money in the world won't bring my boy back. Now we're concerned about our 24-year-old daughter. She's starting to get nosebleeds."

A more-fortunate fallout victim, if you can call her that, is Ilene Provstagaard—a spunky, attractive 28-year-old receptionist. While attending junior and senior high school, Provstagaard and her classmates were frequently escorted to the gymnasium for physical examinations without ever being told why. Doctors gave them glasses of water to drink, then felt their throats for thyroid nodules or precancerous growths—a common symptom of possible radiation damage. A later study by the U.S. Public Health Service showed that thyroid cancers in Utah cities from 1948 to 1962 were 120% above the national average. As an adult, Provstagaard has had thyroid problems for years.

"My thyroid is overactive, causing a lot of shakiness, real-dry skin, frequent bowel movements and so much nausea that I'm always having tests to make sure that I'm not pregnant," she says. "I took pills for three years to slow me down, but they started getting me real dizzy. So then I went on Valium. Nowadays, when I get a cold, it lingers an unusually long time."

Like other residents of St. George, she tries to remain good-natured about her misfortune. "The only time I was really angry was two years ago, when my dad, Orvil Wardle, died of cancer," she says.

"He was a robust man of 48. One night, while he was baby-sitting for my daughter, he said, 'I'm really getting old. I ache all over.' The doctor found a little spot on his lungs and said he'd be dead before Christmas, Unfortunately, he was correct. It was three months of torture watching Daddy shrivel to 90 pounds and die. We had to give him morphine all the time and even smuggled in laetrile.

"It didn't seem fair. He'd already watched his mother die of glandular cancer, which is pretty surely caused by radiation. Daddy wasn't a man of many words, but near the end I asked him what he thought caused his condition. He said, 'I remember the bombs.' He had worked in road construction and was always outside in the dirt."

Maxine Smith's husband, Harley, worked all week at the Nevada Test Site for five years in the 1950s, coming home to his wife and children only on weekends. "One night in June 1970 Harley started quivering all over," she recalls. "The whole bed shook for ten minutes. He told me he'd done that once before at the test site. That's when I first got suspicious. We took him to the doctor, who thought it was just a hernia. The next January, Harley got really sick, and they said it was a tumor. He died later that year. I had to get a job to try to keep the family together."

Part of that family was Maxine's daughter, Kelle, then 11 years old. "She was the baby and the apple of Harley's eye," her mother remembers. "Every weekend the two of them would ride horses together. Her father taught her to love those animals. After he died, she transferred all of her fondness to boys. She became pregnant, married her teenaged lover at 16 and before long was divorced. Many years later I said to her: 'If Daddy'd been alive, he would have killed that boy.' Kelle replied, 'If Daddy'd been alive, I'd still be involved with horses instead of boys.' "

Residual difficulties also plagued 26-year-old Jeff Bradshaw, whose mother had been exposed to Dirty Harry six months before Jeff was born. In high school he was an all-star baseball, football and basketball player and had just received an athletic scholarship to Arizona State University when he came down with an illness diagnosed as Hodgkin's disease. A long, painful series of chemotherapy treatments followed. "The last six years of my life have been ruined," he says. "I just got over my last treatment. The first time they said I was 99% cured. The second time it was 95%. This time they didn't say. I can't even play softball anymore. The one time I tried, the ball hit me in the face and paralyzed my eye."

Nevertheless, Jeff's present mental attitude is positive. He works at his father's car dealership and has been married for a year. But at the beginning he didn't know whether he could handle his illness, "I had a very low opinion of myself," he admits. "I went from accidentally getting addicted to all the medication I had to take to doing it on purpose. It got to where I felt better hooked on painkillers and tranquilizers. I think I'm off everything now. But I am still bitter."

No wonder. Jeff's mother recently required surgery to remove a cancerous breast.

Janet Gordon, another St. George resident, hopes to open offices soon that will offer moral support to surviving radiation victims. "I'm very angry, hurt and confused," she says. "I'll never forget all those years we had to go through thinking that God didn't love us and that's why He was taking our loved ones. What made it even worse was finding out it was *not* God, but the Atomic Energy Commission *playing* God. They knowingly lied to us.

"If the winds shifted toward the big cities," she continues, "they canceled the tests. But when the winds were blowing in our direction, they went right ahead—without any concern for human life or welfare. I've been all over southern Utah, and there's no town where you can walk down the main street without finding a family that hasn't been affected by cancer. It's terribly depressing."

Back in the '50s Gordon's brother, Kent Carroll, was rounding up cattle near St. George on the day a heavy atomic blast was detonated. "He came home that day, vomiting and coughing, saying the dust was hanging like a fog," she recalls. "The horse he'd been riding died a few weeks after Kent died 19 years ago at the age of 27. He'd just finished his master's-degree program and was engaged to be married."

Elizabeth Bruhn Catalan is a 38-year-old schoolteacher who grew up in St. George but now lives in Salt Lake City. One of the most outspoken radiation victims, she formed Citizens Call in Utah, which in November will sponsor hearings designed to publicize the tragic results of nuclear fallout. Her father and a sister were both radiation victims.

On Christmas Eve 1963 Mrs. Catalan and her sister Kay arrived from Los Angeles to visit their father, the president of Dixie Junior College in St. George. "At 43 he was in the prime of his life, a large man with an insatiable intellect and love of the outdoors," she remembers. "The moment we walked in the kitchen door, we knew something was drastically wrong. Daddy's skin had a sickly yellow cast to it. He had lost an alarming amount of weight. He shuffled when he walked. Our family doctor had been there that morning. The tests were conclusive: leukemia. The disease was progressing so fast that he had a month, perhaps two months, left to live. But he managed six months, using the time to prepare us and the college for when he would no longer be around.

"There is nothing graceful about dying from leukemia," Mrs. Catalan goes on. "His intestinal tract was pitted with ulcers. Hematomas were under the surface of his skin, all over. The pain never ceased. New medications would help for a while, then lose their effectiveness, leaving new complications. Daddy died July 4, 1964. Through it all, my father felt sure his disease had been triggered in some way by the nuclear testing. He recalled the day he had been horseback riding out in the desert with three friends when a 'cloud' drifted overhead from a test detonated without warning that morning. He had commented, 'It is like a cloud of doom.' Of the four men present that day, three have died of cancer in some form, as have hundreds of their neighbors."

Mrs. Catalan's youngest sister, Marilyn, died in the 1960s after a choking attack caused by an enlarged thyroid goiter that made it difficult for her to breathe. "All I've ever wanted in my life is to be a mother," says Mrs. Catalan. "I was pregnant in 1967 and lost the baby six months into the pregnancy. Now I keep getting calls from former school classmates who've had three, four, even six miscarriages. One poor woman lost eight babies. Only recently have they made the connection between the AEC's testing and their miscarriages. It's an unending horror story. There are days I think I can't handle one more tragic phone call or letter."

Ironically, it is possible that a familiar symbol of American might was also affected by the fallout. During the midst of the 1955 testing program John Wayne spent 30 days on a St. George location, filming his role as Genghis Khan in *The Conqueror*. Wayne died last year of cancer. So did his co-star, Susan Hayward, in 1975. Cancer also claimed *Conqueror* director Dick Powell in 1963. Ten of the wranglers used as extras and technical advisers on the film succumbed to the same disease.

Human beings weren't the only ones contaminated. In the spring of 1953 more than 4,000 sheep that stood grazing near St. George during the testing died suddenly. Many lambs were born with defects. Local ranchers said they'd never seen similar symptoms, and immediately suspected radiation. Two of them sued the government. But Uncle Sam claimed that the sheep died from a combination of factors including malnutrition, poor management and adverse weather conditions. The ranchers lost the case.

Cattle were also afflicted by fallout. "Twice a day the truck from our dairy cooperative rumbled past my home, unknowingly bringing radioactive milk from our cows, which grazed downwind from the test site," Mrs. Catalan says, thinking back to the early '50s. "That milk went into Las Vegas for processing and distribution throughout Nevada."

Twenty-seven years later, two bills calling for compensation for atomic-testing victims in Utah and Nevada are making their way through the U.S. Senate and the House of Representatives. Senator Edward Kennedy (Dem.-Massachusetts) is sponsoring one of them. "No legislation can completely rectify the wrongs that have been committed against this group of American citizens," Kennedy says. "However, this [bill] attempts to do all that can be done 20 years after the fact."

The governors of Utah, Nevada and even Arizona—a small area of the last was sprinkled by fallout from the tests—are calling for a $17-million, five-year study of the dangers atomic testing poses to public health. Earlier this year a specially appointed task force issued a report to President Jimmy Carter on possible courses of action. Significantly, this was the first time a governmental body admitted partial responsibility for the testing aftermath.

"We may reasonably assume that at least some additional cases of cancer in the downwind population resulted from atmospheric fallout," the report said, choosing its words carefully. But it continued, "From an overall public-health perspective, the added risk to the downwind population from fallout was very small."

Meanwhile, interested individuals were awaiting trial of *Allen et al.* v. *the U.S.,* the multimillion-dollar lawsuit. Former Interior Secretary Stuart Udall is one of four attorneys representing the claimants. "I was brought into the case by people I know in that area of southern Utah," he says. "They felt a great wrong had been done. The more I investigated, the more monstrous it became. The case could easily stand as a landmark. That's why the government doesn't want to open a Pandora's box."

Washington agencies do indeed seem uneasy. In its February 1980 report to President Carter the Interagency Task Force on Compensation for Radiation-Related Illnesses said: "Litigation of these claims carries with it the risk of establishing judicial precedents which could be harmful to the government in other radiation and toxic-substance litigation. Any adverse ruling on that issue would have precedential impact upon other occupational and environmental-pollution cases."

William G. Schaffer, who supervised that task force, is also heading the government's legal case in *Allen et al.* v. *the U.S.* He says the report to the President—which includes scientists' testimony that cancers cannot be linked with prior radiation—is currently "under study." He feels the government's case in the lawsuit will reflect the same conclusion.

"It's fair to assume our position wouldn't differ," says Schaffer. "As for the case's being a bad precedent, I'll only say that bad cases make bad law, and this is a pretty unusual lawsuit."

In the meantime, past and present residents of St. George quietly go on living—and dying. The more-skeptical survivors wonder why 35 local citizens were invited last year by the Department of Energy—successor to the Atomic Energy Commission—on a two day tour of the Nevada Test Site, where only underground tests are now being conducted. Strangely, the Energy Department provided large quantities of booze for its predominantly Mormon guests, apparently unaware that their religion forbids them to consume alcoholic beverages.

"They treated us like we were the President," says one who made the trip. "They fed us lobster and filet mignon, and they had a huge cocktail party. Can you imagine *that* for a group of Mormons? All of us were asking if we could have Sprite, the soft drink, instead. It seemed like one big PR job to make us go back home and tell our friends that everything out there on the testing site was under control."

Dave Miller explains the Energy Department's position: "It was public relations in the sense of informing them about what we're doing now with underground tests. We also wanted to remind them that there really was an honest attempt in the 1950s to stay within the levels of exposure standards that existed in those days."

While most of the people of St. George feel that the worst is over and that testing is now safe, a movement is under way among the more-militant radiation victims to abandon the desert test site. "I want to see it closed down before it kills anyone else," says Preston Truman, a 28-year-old cancer victim attempting to end all testing in Nevada. "I've found people who say there have been up to 40 radiation leaks since 1963, the year that the Nuclear Test Ban Treaty went into effect. At times, off-site monitoring systems have not even been turned on during testing. Yet the Energy Department says monitoring systems indicated there was no radiation present.

"One of my biggest gripes is that the U.S. isn't content with just blowing up its own bombs in Nevada. We also have to invite Britain to test theirs.

"Nonsense," says Dave Miller. "We haven't had a ventilator [release of radiation] since 1970. The cornerstone of our nation's defense posture is a credible nuclear deterrent, and we can't have that deterrent unless we can test. As for the monitoring systems, some of those off-site aren't handled by us—so we can't take full responsibility. As for the British, we have an agreement with the United Kingdom to test their devices. They *are* our allies, aren't they?"

Truman insists that one recent underground test was delayed 24 hours to wait for the winds to shift away from heavily populated areas—the same step that proved fatal for St. George in the past. "We're told all is safe there now, he says. "But we've heard that one before."

In the meantime he continues fighting his own lymphatic cancer. "I've been in remission since 1973; so I just sit, and hope each day that passes won't be my last," Truman reflects. "I've talked to many of my former classmates recently and couldn't believe the number of their kids' birth defects and their own sterility cases. That's particularly sad in a state like Utah, which places such heavy emphasis on the family and future generations."

Others besides the federal government are uncomfortable with the cries of protest coming from St. George, especially the city manager and the Chamber of Commerce. They're concerned that the negative publicity might eventually hurt tourism. Each year more than 2 million travelers pass through Washington County—the gateway to Zion National Park. St. George attracts more than 10,000 conventioneers annually.

"I've said the government should go beyond reimbursement and provide an apology to the people here," maintains Arthur Anderson, seated in his Chamber of Commerce Building office. But curiously, Anderson's sentiments in a letter to lawyer Stuart Udall were steeped in compromise: "Why don't we move off the idea that money salves all wounds and, though it may sound facetious, ask the President of the United States instead to come out to Utah and apologize on behalf of an errant but grateful government?"

Anderson also points out that despite "an effort by the media to put out a gloom-and-doom story," tourism in St. George had its biggest year in 1979, and shows no signs of abating.

"I'm a little concerned that some may get the wrong idea because a minority speaks louder than the majority," says City Manager Gary Esplin. "Victims have a right to seek a solution to their problems. But the city's position is not to take a stand on the lawsuit, because we represent *all* the people of St. George, many of them new residents who have no connection with the testing and its aftermath."

John Rogers, general manager of the daily *Color Country Spectrum*, agrees that St. George's name has been tainted. "When I tell people where I'm from, they immediately link St. George with radiation," he admits. "But our community is growing anyhow, and most knowledgeable people realize we don't have a radiation problem anymore."

Utah Governor Scott Matheson puts the radiation issue in perspective. "The reasons for finally resolving all the questions about the health impact of the fallout are not limited to what it will do for people of this region," he says.

"If this nation is to allow additional growth of nuclear power as a major way of reducing our reliance upon imported oil," Matheson continues, "then the health of the nation will be fundamentally determined by the answers we receive. ... We cannot afford to wait another 30 years to find out if we are exposing large numbers of our citizens to hazards that will continue to affect them for generations to come."

While most of the claimants in the *Allen et al.* v. *the U.S.* lawsuit feel that the worst clouds of danger have passed, they are no longer the wide-eyed patriots of the past. Nor do they maintain the blind faith in government that they once did. "I feel used," says Elizabeth Catalan. "We did what we were asked to do by the government. The community went all out. And in return we were conned. They knew of the dangers, but they chose not to tell us. We had a right to know."

After all these years Mrs. Catalan has barely learned to live with the fear of who will be the next to die, and when. "Unless citizens take action, what happened in St. George can happen anywhere else," she says. "There's only one logical response to such a possibility—never again!"

———————————

This was the fire storm I was born into. I had multiple birth defects. A cleft palate, a double cleft upper lip, a deformed nose, and my upper jawbone was in three pieces instead of one. My first surgery was done when I was six weeks old. My younger sister was born a year and a half later with a single cleft lip. My older sister, Tamara Lucetta Anderson, or Tami, was born before the testing and was born normal. My younger sister was Sandra Sue Anderson, or Sandy.

CHAPTER 2

ILLINOIS

Some of my first memories were when we lived in Illinois. My dad worked for the department of agriculture in Chicago. We lived in the suburbs in a town called Park Forest. I went to Lakewood elementary school. My dad signed me up for peanut league baseball in 1964. I was socially awkward with my speech impediment and my facial deformities. When people first looked at me, their nose would scrunch up, and their eyes would get big. Their eyebrows would go up. I call it "the look." I could tell what they were thinking. It was like "ewwe, what happened to your face"? Some people would ask if I had been in a car accident. The other kids were cruel and laughed at me. I think I dealt with this by excelling in sports and other school activities. My grades in school were very good. Sometimes they would pull me out of a class to work with a speech therapist, but my speech never got better because of my cleft palate and my upper jawbone being separated. The two clefts in my upper lip went clear through my upper jawbone. If you grabbed my two front teeth, you could wiggle the whole front of my upper jaw. They called it a "mobile pre-maxilla ".

I remember my dad got me a Schwinn stingray bicycle and I would ride for miles to my baseball games and practices, with my baseball glove looped onto the handlebars. I made friends with my team, and I loved playing baseball! I wore out many sets of tires on that bike and I loved doing daredevil stunts on it. One time I was showing off and

I pedaled so fast that I accidentally pedaled backwards which applied the brakes. I flew over the handlebars and split my chin open on the sidewalk. I had to get about 10 stitches in my chin.

Then there was the day that I was walking home from school with a couple of my friends. As we passed the Catholic school, I bragged that I could throw a rock over the school. I gave it my best try, but the rock went through a classroom window. A large nun came running out of the school. My friends ran away, but I stayed to face the consequences. She marched me into her office, and I thought I would get beaten with a ruler. Luckily, she didn't beat me, but she called my dad and told him about the incident. When I got home, I thought I would be severely punished, but my dad had a new baseball glove for me, for being honest, and fessing up to it. I still had to work to pay for the window. I seem to have been born with moral values, or my dad instilled that in me at a very young age.

And I remember very little of my mother. She had separated from my dad and was living somewhere else. One day, I rode my bike to our old neighborhood and saw my mom there. I hadn't seen her in quite a while. I remember she picked me up and sat me on the counter. She asked me how I got the stitches in my eyebrow, and I explained that I bumped heads with a kid in school. I asked her to come back home, but she said she couldn't. I remember being very hurt. It seemed like a few months later, when my dad sat me and my two sisters down and told us that our mother had passed away. He wouldn't tell us what happened, and we would never know until we researched it as adults. She was shot by her boyfriend, who then shot himself.

I often wondered what it would be like to have a mom. My dad would hire different babysitters to watch us, and he would go on business trips that would last a week. It seems like we had a dad on Saturdays and Sundays but that was it. One babysitter was a black woman who seemed to only cook hotdogs. Another was an older white woman who spoiled us with sweets. We also stayed with neighbors, and we got shuffled around a lot. I remember a picnic in the neighborhood where I got a marshmallow stuck in my throat. A nice lady with long fingernails got it out. I am pretty sure she saved my life. My brushes with death would become a common occurrence in my life.

I had frequent plastic surgeries in Chicago, and that city just looked gray and smoky to me. I remember hearing the Beach Boys on the car radio. About that time, President Kennedy was assassinated.

I loved to climb trees and racked up a few more injuries doing that. I jumped out of a tree and ended up with a golf tee stuck in my heel. I had to go to the hospital and have it removed. I loved reading Spider-Man and other comic books. I wish I would have kept those. I had some of the first comic books ever made. I had a good friend named Samir. I think his parents were from India. We would play marbles, we had cap guns, and we collected and traded baseball cards.

I have always loved to learn, and I would ride my bicycle to the library and read for hours. The Beatles became popular, and my sisters and I would buy their latest records. We wore them out on the record player. I also had a transistor radio that would hang on the handlebars of my bicycle. I spent most of my time riding my bike all over town. My dad would be out of town every week til the weekend, and we had very little parental supervision. My neighbors had a Buick Wildcat and I thought it was the coolest thing I'd ever seen! I started to build model cars about this time. I had a good friend name Todd, who was very intelligent, and liked to learn like me.

My dad dated a couple women and there was one that I liked very much. She was a fourth-grade teacher and had a son named Alex. I guess she and my dad didn't hit it off. Then he met my future step-mother, Ida. Right off the bat, I didn't like her. She was mean spirited, dishonest, and abusive. I did find out later that she was schizophrenic. After she married my dad, the abuse got worse. She would beat my sisters and I with a big wooden spaghetti spoon. Ida's parents lived in Chicago Heights, Illinois, and they were straight from Italy. It was torturous to visit them, but they did make some good spaghetti.

In fourth grade, I had a crush on my teacher, Miss Flaschen. Maybe part of it was that I needed a mother figure in my life. I was heartbroken when she got married and became Mrs. Beck.

Dear Aunt Etta,

This picture was taken of the kids by Bob this summer & I'm ashamed of the dirty arms & faces, ~~but they are in~~ their most

THIS IS A
KODACOLOR ENLARGEMENT
Made by Kodak

DECEMBER 1960 · RB

natural make up. They are such wonderful children & I think their dispositions shine thru in this picture.

Thank you so much for your Christmas gift. I hope you know how much we appreciate it.

We hope your Christmas & the coming year will be as happy as ours!

Love,
Nancy

CHAPTER 3

NEW JERSEY

Since my dad worked for the government, we got transferred several times. First Utah, then Illinois, and now, New Jersey. My dad worked across the river in Philadelphia. I was still going through many surgeries and orthodontics, to repair my birth defects. I spent some time in Saint Christopher's hospital for children in Philadelphia, and I would ride the bus to Philadelphia by myself at 12 years old to see the orthodontist. I endured so many painful sessions of having my braces tightened to straighten my two front teeth. All this torture turned out to be a waste of time when the surgeons pulled out my two front teeth to do a bone graft, which would solidify my upper jaw. Then the plan was to install an eight-piece bridge. The orthodontist had been trying to straighten two front teeth that were connected to a floating section of the bone. To pull the teeth required a tool that split them apart from between the teeth. I even had to wear the metal band around my head with elastic across the back of my head.

Here I was in a new state, trying to make new friends, while people made fun of me because of my parents and my speech impediment. I tried to ignore it, but it was very emotionally painful. I didn't look people in the eyes because I didn't want to see what they were thinking. I had a couple more surgeries on the roof of my mouth that were unsuccessful. During one of my nose surgeries, they packed both my nostrils with long gauze strips, treated with pharmaceutical cocaine. I would wake up after surgery high as a kite. I remember catching a second buzz when they removed them. At the time I didn't know what it was but years later, experimenting with cocaine, I recognized the taste. After the nose surgeries, I would have two black eyes from them breaking my nose. People would ask me who punched me, or other comments. After surgeries on my upper lip, I could not smile, or I would break the stitches. I would have to physically hold my face if something made me laugh. Another bad thing was no solid foods after mouth surgery. Once, I was in the hospital, and they brought in a tray of really good food, but then they switched it for a tray of Jell-O and soft foods. I was thoroughly disappointed! I also had one appointment with an oral surgeon. He removed about five teeth that were growing in where there shouldn't be any teeth. This was done with local anesthesia while I was awake. I walked out of there with my whole body shaking.

There were a lot of good times in New Jersey too. We lived in Willingboro, a suburb of Philadelphia. The town was divided into parks. We lived in Hawthorne Park, where all the street names began with an H. We lived at 27 Harper Lane. Each park had an identical grade school with a swimming pool. Our pool had a high diving board and a little one. I started out with regular dives and cannon balls. Soon, I was doing one and a half flips off the low dive, and then the high dive. I must've been hitting puberty because the lifeguards were smokin' hot! They would lay on their towels with their transistor radios, playing the awesome music of the 60s.

There are certain moments in my life that seem to stick in my mind like video that never fades away. One of these moments was when I was arriving at the pool, and a very beautiful girl, who was laying on a towel in her bikini with her little radio playing. The song was "Make it With You", by Bread. I think I fell in love with girls and guitar music in the same moment!

THE AMERICAN ASSOCIATION FOR HEALTH, PHYSICAL EDUCATION, AND RECREATION

A DEPARTMENT OF THE NATIONAL EDUCATION ASSOCIATION

YOUTH FITNESS
ACHIEVEMENT AWARD

FITNESS FOR YOUTH

PRESENTED TO

ROBERT ANDERSON

in recognition of physical fitness proficiency
demonstrated by meeting the national standards
established by the AAHPER Youth Fitness Project.

SIGNED THIS *1st* DAY OF *June*

TEST ADMINISTRATOR

WILLIAMSBURG MEMORIAL
SCHOOL OR AGENCY

JUNIOR DIVISION

Carl A. Troester, Jr.
Executive Secretary
AAHPER

Sam M. Lambert
Executive Secretary
NEA

Of course, I had a cool bicycle that I rode all over town, and I would build a ramp to jump over stacks of tires. I could ride a wheelie all the way down my street. I was playing Little League baseball, and I was very good at it. I guess at that time I had been playing for five or six years. Baseball taught me a lot about winning, losing, and sportsmanship. My dad would always say, it's not whether you win or lose, it's how you play the game. In 1969, I was chosen by every team coach to be on the All-Star team. I had a black friend on my team named Greg, who was also chosen. He was a home run hitter, and very talented. We won a few games, and we were getting close to the state championships, but I had another stroke of bad luck. I broke the two middle fingers of my right hand.

On my 12th birthday, I was old enough to have a paper route, and I signed up. I put baskets on my bike and delivered about 50 papers a day. I would stop at the store and buy tasty cakes and other food that we weren't allowed to have. I think I brought a few home to my sisters. I had a cigar box that I would keep my money in.

When my father would leave for work during the week, we were only allowed to drink so much milk each day. When my dad was home, my stepmother would make a big pot of spaghetti. In the evenings, my dad and Ida would sit at the picnic table on the back porch and talk. She would tell him lies about us, and we could hear everything because our bedroom windows were right above the porch. We would confront our dad with her lies, and her abuse, but he wasn't much help. He would always say "try to understand that she has problems". If we left a bedroom light on, she would beat us with the spoon.

One day she was beating my sisters in the next room, and their screaming set me off. I barged into the room, grabbed her spoon, and broke it in half. Then I grabbed her by the arms and slammed her against the wall with her feet off the ground. She looked at me with disbelief and shock since I had always been peaceful until I had enough. I believe I got grounded and disciplined by my dad, but that was the end of the wooden spoon beatings.

I was very interested in cars during this time, and I still am today. My neighbor had a 69 Chevelle Super Sport. In our neighborhood, there was also a GTO Judge and a Plymouth Road Runner. It was a golden age for cars and for music! My dad would take me to Atco Dragway in Atco, New Jersey. I had a good friend named David down the street. Their family was into the hippie culture and wore bell bottom pants, tie-dyes, etc. We had to wear straight leg pants and I had to have short hair. David's sister had a boyfriend that went to Vietnam.

I was a couple years too young to get drafted. Her boyfriend Ed was such a great guy but came back from the war a changed man.

My dad went to buy a new car at the Chevy dealership. There was a 69 Camaro pace car on the showroom floor. It was white with orange stripes and the price was $3500. I told my dad to buy it, but he bought a brown Impala. Today the Camaro is worth over $150,000!

Ida was one of the worst drivers I've ever seen. She would be on the freeway and downshift the automatic transmission to slow down instead of hitting the brakes. Once, she backed out of the post office without looking right into oncoming traffic. A girl in a 67 Lemans slammed into our passenger side. My head banged off the door window, and the girl in the other car was furious! I had a big lump on my right temple. We were originally Methodist, but Ida converted us all to Catholics. We were baptized, then communion, then confirmation. We had to walk about 3 miles to church, and then catechism. Somebody chose "Victor" as my confirmation name. After catechism, my sisters and I would walk all the way back home. We would be starving but weren't allowed to eat until about 6 PM when the spaghetti was ready.

One of my favorite hobbies was building model cars. I had quite a collection until Ida smashed them. Once I was in the hospital, they let me build a model. It was called "The Visible V-8". It was a complex model of a working V-8 engine. It was made of clear plastic so you could see all the working parts rotating inside of it. It even has spark plugs that lit up on the power stroke.

Eventually, I graduated grade school and went to Willingboro Memorial junior high school. We had racial riots and police in the hallways. The population was about 50% black 40% white and 10% mixed. I never had issues with people unless they messed with my older sister. She was very pretty, and guys would hit on her. I remember the routine, "meet me at the flagpole after school dude". Usually they wouldn't show up, but one day I was delivering papers on my bike, and a gang of them threw me off a bridge. Bicycle, papers, and all, into about 6 inches of water. I only had bruises from that one. I managed to gather up my papers while they laughed at me.

During junior high, students underwent a weeklong test called STEP and SCAT. There was a whole day of each subject. When the results came in, I was told that I came in second out of 5,000 students in the whole school. My friend, Bruce, was first. My score for social studies was a bit low, but I had no interest in history. My total score was 98 to 99.

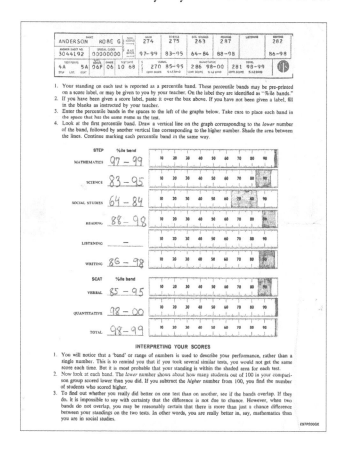

I also underwent a complete assessment before one of my surgeries. I remember seeing a form on the dining room table from the assessment. It described my mental health as "terrible". I remember a woman, showing me the cards with blotches on them and asking me what I see in them. Looking back, she was probably right. I felt sadness from losing my mom, anger at several different things, social anxiety, extreme shyness, and other issues. The only bright spots in my life were my sisters, my few friends, sports, music, and cars. I also loved to hike in the woods nearby, and I made a lot of rope swings and tree houses. My favorite role model was Spider-Man. Maybe because he was bitten by a radioactive spider.

The 60s was such a beautiful time! The TV shows had moral values, and they were truly funny without vulgarity or violence. People hitchhiked without worrying about serial killers. Children played outside till dark or until the streetlights came on. The ice cream truck was a special treat, if you had a dime or a quarter. I would buy the latest Beatles or CCR records at the store. There was, however, unrest over the Vietnam war.

I was playing wiffleball with some neighbors in our yard, and I broke the two middle fingers of my right hand. I was sliding into second base, which was a sewer top, and as I slid in hands first someone stepped on my fingers. I knew right away they were broken, and I ran into the house. Ida (I called her Ida instead of stepmother, or step monster) put two Band-Aids on my fingers even though they weren't bleeding.

Then she took me to see my baseball coach, when I wanted to go to the hospital. My dad was out of town, and I think Ida was more concerned about my baseball coach than my fingers. He told her to take me to the hospital where they reset my fingers by pulling them and then splinted them. I had to miss the All-Star games and we lost the second or third game. That meant we were done.

All during this time, Ida was pocketing our grocery money and buying the cheapest food that she could. I mostly ate the cheapest peanut butter and jelly that she could find. She would buy powdered milk in a big box and mix it with tap water. Then she put lines on the milk jug. We were only allowed to drink a small amount of the powdered instant milk each day.

My dad took me to Atco Dragway about five times, and I loved the races! He would take pictures of the races. The first ones were black and white and then color. His hobby was photography. We saw nitro methane burning dragsters and funny cars. They would do the quarter mile in about six seconds at over 200 mph. I think a person has to actually be there to appreciate the intensity of these cars. The smell of the nitro and burning rubber, and the sound of these cars that literally shakes your bones!

During this time, my dad and I were bonding a little bit, but we were never very close, and I don't think either one of us ever showed our feelings. I can't recall my dad ever saying he loved me or my sisters. He was kind of a robotic, drill sergeant type. I really wish he didn't take his orders from Ida. I moved up from Little League to Babe Ruth league, and I loved playing baseball. If I would have pursued a career as a baseball player, I could have been very successful. My coaches wanted me to move up to the minor leagues, but my dad got transferred again to DC, and we moved to Va.

I was also on the wrestling team in NJ, and my coach gave me a youth fitness achievement award.

CHAPTER 4

VIRGINIA

Since my dad worked for the department of agriculture, he was being transferred for the third time. He was promoted to assistant national supervisor in DC. We moved to a suburb of DC, Fairfax, Virginia.

Here we go again, my sisters, and I had to make new friends and start a new life. The town had a southern atmosphere to it. The streets and townships were named after Civil War generals. The high school football team was called the Fairfax Rebels. Their mascot was Johnny Reb.

Starting new schools was hard for me. Every year I would tell myself, "I'm going to meet a nice girl this year and I'll have a girlfriend". It never would happen though. I had a friend next-door named Donald. I'll leave out his last name because he wasn't the sharpest knife in the drawer. In metal shop, he lit the torch with it aimed at his hand. After school, he got in the driver seat of the school bus and turned the ignition key. The bus started up and hit the next bus in line, which then hit the next bus in line. Luckily, nobody was in between the buses.

One day I found an engine in the woods, and I was so excited to take it apart. I went home and got my box of tools and rolled it on the seat of my bicycle to where the engine was. On the way back a car pulled up next to me and six black guys got out.

They looked like basketball players. They were all more than 6 feet tall. They stole my toolbox and drove away. My wallet was in the toolbox with $18 in it. I got the tag number and called the cops. They said they would catch them, but I never heard anything back.

I built a few go-carts and I would ride them around the neighborhood streets. One neighbor at the bottom of my street would call the cops on us. One night we planned our revenge on this neighbor and planted firecrackers all around his house. We wrapped the fuse into a cigarette for about a three-minute fuse then we watched from my friend's house across the street. We watched the neighbor run in and out of his house about five times. It was hilarious!

My neighbors on the other side were a German family. I'll leave out their last name. There was Jay and his sister Johanna. I kind of had a crush on Johanna. I had a crush on every girl in the neighborhood. There was a beautiful, blonde girl halfway down my street that had a candy apple red 55 Chevy. She was about five years older than me, and she was the goddess of the neighborhood.

One day, Jay and I found a big can of gun powder in his dad's basement. We rigged up a canning jar, half full of powder with a fuse through the top. We buried it a little in the center of my backyard and lit the fuse. We definitely weren't expecting to blow a 3-foot-wide crater in my backyard! There were neighbors all running around, trying to figure out what it happened. We acted like we didn't have a clue, and we somehow got away with it. I had to fill in a lot of dirt, fill the crater, and destroy the evidence.

Another stunt I pulled was the underground fort that I dug against the backside of the house. It was in a corner where the chimney went up and I had it covered with a sheet of plywood with grass on top. About a year later, my dad found it and thought it was a bomb shelter. My sisters and I thought that was funny as hell, and we never told him differently.

I got a job at Mosby Woods Mobil. I started out pumping gas. In those days it was full service, and I would wash the windows and check tire pressure, check the oil, etc. I became a mechanic at the age of 14.

One night, a regular customer came in for gas. He was an army lieutenant, and he drove a Volkswagen beetle. He asked me if I wanted a ride home and said he had some beer. I started to drink at that age, and I agreed. As he was driving me home and I was drinking a beer, he went past the turn for my house. I told him that he passed my house and he said he was going to get more beer. He got on to Chain Bridge Road, (123) and started heading out of town. Then he put his right hand on my crotch, and I knew I was in trouble. The last civilization before leaving Fairfax was the hospital on the left side of the road. I weighed all my options in about two seconds. Then I downshifted his car and jumped out at about 50 miles an hour. After that it seems like everything happened in slow motion. I landed on my back and slid on the asphalt. It seemed like I slid forever, and I finally came to a stop.

I was still conscious, and I looked up to see him backing up towards me. I still remember the loud, whining sound of the beetle backing up towards me at full speed. Somehow, I got up on my feet and ran into the trees on the side of the road. I went far enough to be in a dark area, and I hid myself and kept very still. I could see him under the streetlight with a gun saying, "come here, you little bastard". He looked for me, but luckily, didn't find me, and his car was in the road so eventually, he left. I was in a daze, or in shock for a while, but I finally got to the hospital. The back of my head was scraped down to my skull. Both of my shoulder blades were scraped bad. My butt cheeks were both scraped off. They did a lot of cleaning and stitching on me and called the police. The cop asked me where it happened, and I told him right out in front of here.

We walked out to Chain Bridge Road, and there was about a 40-foot red stripe down the road. There was blood, hair, shirt, and pants fragments, etc. The cop was speechless at the scene. I told him who did it, and that it was a white VW with red pinstripes. The cops caught him at 5 AM, going into a hotel room with another guy. Maybe the lieutenant should have kept his hands off THIS 14-year-old!

I missed a day of school recovering from this, and they wrote me a pass for missing school. One of my teachers didn't believe that my pass was real, and she called me up to the front of the class. As she looked at my pass, the whole class could see the back of my head was scraped off and stitched up. The teacher changed her tune when I walked back to my seat.

My dad really ticked me off when he didn't press charges. He seemed to think military people were above the law. I think he just wasn't a take charge type of person. Maybe that's why our stepmother wore the pants in our family. All this added to the fact that I was an angry young man.

I had another surgery at Sibley Memorial Hospital in DC. Sometimes they would work on my nose, sometimes my cleft palate, sometimes my lip, and once it was bone grafts in my upper jaw. I won't mention my surgeon's name because I don't have anything good to say about him. I always hoped to come out looking like a regular person, but it never happened. I remember what the doctor would say, "wait for the swelling to go down and you'll be looking great!" This particular surgery was worse than the rest. When I woke up, my dad was sitting in the hospital room. I felt nauseated, and I moved over to the side of the bed and vomited at least a gallon of blood all over the floor. My dad called the nurse, and they cleaned it up. Apparently, my stomach filled up with blood when they broke my nose. When I got home, I noticed a needle mark and a sore spot by my heart. I felt like I had been beaten up bad. I had an explosive temper for some reason, and my hair was falling out in chunks. I'm pretty sure I died on the operating table, and they brought me back. I felt like death warmed over. My long blonde hair was the only thing that looked good about me, and it was falling out. I remember smashing a few things, and I think this was largely due to the drugs they gave me.

To this day, my hair loss has never changed from then. It never got worse, but it never grew back either. Working at Mosby Woods Mobil was an adventure in itself. We had quite a colorful crew! The owner was Andy. He had a son, Scott, who worked there occasionally. Scott was a funny guy with long hair and was into drugs of all kinds. I think he was high on pot most of the time.

There were two brothers, Art, and Roger. Art was kind of a stern, southern boy with his pointy toed cowboy boots. Roger was about the meekest person I've ever met. He never cursed or did anything wrong. He got the nickname "Sheesh" because he could bust a knuckle wrenching on a car, and all he would say was "sheesh!". There was always country music playing on the radio in the shop. It was great classic country then like Patsy Cline, Johnny Cash, Hank Williams, etc. There were two mechanics, Jim, and Dave. They both taught me a lot. Jim was an awesome mechanic, and he did everything with one arm. He had polio as a child and his right arm had very little movement. Dave was a little older. He had no front teeth and he drank whiskey every day after the boss, Andy, went home. There was a young guy,

Albert, who pumped gas, and another guy, Bill Wilson, who pumped gas as well. Bill was a huge guy and he should have been a comedian. One day, a girl pulled in with a flat tire, and Bill lifted the back end of the car while I changed the tire. In those days, gas stations were full service. We would wash the windshield and the back window, and ask if they wanted the oil checked, etc. Andy thought he was God's gift to women, and he would swagger out to a lady's car and flirt with her. My stepmother would come in with the Impala and flirt with Andy. She wore her culotte shorts, and I wouldn't be surprised if she cheated on my dad.

We had lively conversation around the garage about women, sex, and other manly topics. The target of most of our jokes was sheesh. And we would ask him if he had ever had sex, and he would just laugh. Andy would tell sheesh that masturbating would make him go blind. Andy would leave around four and Dave would get his fifth of whiskey out from under his car seat. We used to joke that he had a four on the floor and a fifth under the seat. People would come in and pick up their cars, and Dave would be drunk and calling their car a piece of shit. It was hilarious! We would assure the customer that he was sober when he fixed it.

There were a couple of memorable incidents while I worked at the mobile station. One day, a big stake body truck pulled into the 7-Eleven next-door. It was full of Christmas trees, and there were about seven or eight migrant workers in the back with the trees. The driver of the truck went in the store and forgot to put the parking brake on. The truck rolled backwards down the parking lot, crossed Plantation Parkway, and hit the curb at about 30 miles an hour. When it hit the curb, I saw migrant workers and Christmas trees flying through the air. The truck went down the embankment as the driver came out of 7-Eleven looking for his truck. Nobody was seriously hurt, and they had to winch the truck out of the ravine.

Another incident was when a guy got gas and I gave him change from a roll of bills that I had carried in my pocket. He parked on the side of 7-Eleven and robbed the place. He only got 50 bucks, and I had about 200 in my pocket. I gave the police a good description of the vehicle. I'm not sure if they ever caught him.

I was taking auto mechanics in high school, and my teacher was Mr. Pritchett. He drove a VW Karman Gia, and one day he was joking around and told me to pull the engine out of his car while he was in a teachers meeting. When he returned to the class an hour later, his engine was on the workbench and I had found a hole in one piston. He kind of freaked out a little because he didn't have a ride home! On the other hand, his car was about halfway fixed. There was a VW dealership in Fairfax called HB Lantsch, and somehow, I got the nickname H.B.

My sister Tammy had just gotten her first car and it was a 58 VW bug. I had the motor out a couple times, and I had VW engine removal down to a science. They were actually pretty easy to do. Cars were simpler then. No electronic ignition, front wheel drive, etc. I was a mechanic at the Mobil station at age 14, but I didn't get paid a mechanic salary, and they sort of kept it quiet.

I had a friend, Jeff, who had a 51 Studebaker that we would work on. One night, Jeff and my neighbor, Johanna, and I all went to the rope swing in Mosby Woods. I'm not sure about them, but I was drinking beer and smoking pot. I had never been to the swing, but I was fearless and ready to show off my daredevil skills. The swing was built into a hill, and the further out you swung, the higher you were off the ground. I had to climb up a second tree and have them swing the rope up to me. When I swung out, I realized I was headed directly towards the main tree that the rope was hanging from. Someone had slid the rope from out on the branch to right up against the tree. I slammed into the tree, my right shoulder hitting the tree, sending me spinning into the darkness, still swinging on the rope. If I bailed off the rope at that point, I would've been slung 50 yards and if I baled while swinging backwards towards the tree, I would've slammed into the side of the hill. Another option was to hit the tree again while spinning. At times like this, it seems that everything happens in slow motion. I considered all my options in less than a second, and I decided to jump when the rope came to a stop at its highest point. I fell about three stories to a hard landing on the ground. I landed on my feet, and my feet were both seriously injured. The worst pain, however, was my private parts from the impact of hitting the ground. I laid there on the ground writhing in pain. Jeff and Johanna ran down the hill to me. I told them to take off my left shoe because I had burst the blood vessels in my left foot, and it was swelling up fast. They helped me up the hill to Jeff's car and took me to Fairfax Hospital. It seems like I waited for hours in excruciating pain. Finally, they x- rayed my left foot and told me it wasn't broken. I was sure that it was. It was purple and about the size of a football!

The next day in school, I passed out in class from the pain. The school had my stepmother, Ida, take me to another doctor. As I waited in the waiting room with Ida and my sister, Sandy, I removed the ace bandages on my foot, and everybody gasped. My foot was still purple and about the same size as a football. They x-rayed it and told me I had shattered several bones and burst the blood vessels. After doing what they could to it, they put a cast on it, and told me to keep it elevated for a few months. They told me I might not be able to walk on it again. If it had been done right to begin with, I would've been in much better shape.

The next few months were hell!. Lying on the living room couch with my foot elevated, listening to Ida, and not being able to escape her. Just the whiny tone of her voice was irritating. And then there was the music she played on the stereo. Jerry Vale, Bing Crosby, etc. it was torture! I slowly got better, and got around on crutches for a while, and I finally walked again. I remember how good it felt to walk again. I developed arthritis in my foot soon after that, and I had to have Cortisone injections in the joints of my foot. Those were so painful, I had tears coming out of my eyes. My left foot is still crooked, and this would be the first of many alcohol related injuries.

CHAPTER 5

JAN

There was a trampoline at a neighbor's house, and all of my friends would hang out there. I was good at doing front flips and backflips from my years in New Jersey, and the high diving board. My foot was healed up enough to engage in more daredevil activities. I had a friend named Kirk who lived in Mosby woods. He was a one-of-a-kind human being. He was small, though he later grew quite tall. He had bright red hair and was a ball of energy. He got the nickname spark plug because of his red hair, and he was the life of the party. His crude humor, and his tough guy attitude was hilarious coming from a small guy. He introduced me to two sisters that lived in his neighborhood, Jan and Carol. He liked Carol but I don't think she thought he was her type. Both Sisters were beautiful girls and I had a crush on Jan. One day I took Jan to the trampoline, mainly because I wanted to show off and impress her.

After a few backflips, front flips, etc., we got a little frisky, wrestling in the grass. I remember having my arms around her and giving her a kiss. The sparks were flying, and I had never experienced this before!

There was not a doubt in my mind I was in love! I loved everything about her. Her girly smile, her beautiful blonde hair, her personality, and the way she made me laugh. We would talk for hours and never run out of things to say. We did a lot of kissing, and I could tell that she wasn't ready for sex. My hands would wander, and she would block my hands. That was fine with me because I loved her and just wanted to be with her. She lived in the apartment or townhouse or whatever they were, in Mosby Woods. We would sit in the breezeway of the buildings and enjoy each other's company for hours. The Mobil station where I worked was only about 100 yards from Jan's house. Sometimes she would ride with me to get Varsol at Fairfax Circle. Every night we would clean the garage floor with Varsol, and I would drive the company truck to get it. It was an old red 63 Chevy pickup with a three speed on the column. I didn't even have a driver's license yet. Jan would scoot over next to me in the truck, and I felt like I had finally found love and happiness. Looking back, there wasn't much love in my life.

I pulled a few other stunts with no driver's license. I was itching to drive, and I would go out in the middle of the night and coast my sister Tami's VW beetle down the hill in neutral, and then start it up and drive around. That way I didn't wake up my parents. My dad slept like a rock from drinking his nightly quarts of Budweiser, but Ida would wake up easily. Putting the car back was a little trickier. I had to fly up the hill with enough speed that I could shut off the engine and coast up the hill to the parking spot. I got away with it every time. My sister Tami was a year and a half older than me, and she got a 70 Camaro and sold me her bug. I would sneak the Camaro out too. It was OK with Tami, she was very understanding of my obsession with cars.

I hung out with Jan as much as possible. She was my number one obsession. My friend, spark plug would be jealous because I didn't hang out with him much anymore. Jan would write me a poem that went straight to my heart. Those were the happiest days of my life.

In school, I hung out with Jan between classes. She was a grade lower than me. I was taking another auto mechanics class with Mr. Bradford as my teacher, and I was really excelling in gymnastics in gym class. I thought I could breeze through auto shop class, but one day Mr. Bradford came into our Mobil station and caught me putting an intake on a 57 dodge power wagon. My whole body was under the hood, and he poked his head in and said is that you Bob? I was busted and he made me an assistant instructor in class. I would show students how to balance tires and other simple tasks.

My gym teacher, Mr. Atherton, told the class if anyone can do this, I will give them an A for a 9 week class. He was talking about hanging from the chin up bar and pulling yourself all the way up without bending your elbows, I guess he thought it was impossible until I did it on the first try. He kept his word and gave me an A. He was also impressed with my gymnastic skills and wanted me to join the gymnastics team. I never did. My schedule was so full with school in the morning and I worked from 3pm till 11 at night.

It was hard to wake up in the morning, but my dad would throw a glass of cold water in my face when I didn't get up on time. I never could figure out how he drank every night and woke up every morning. One morning he found my baggie of pot on my dresser. I had forgotten to hide it when I fell asleep. I caught the third-degree on that one! He called it dope. I later found it in the trashcan and substituted a baggie of Ida's oregano. It was buried under all his empty quart bottles.

This was the time in my life where there was so much going on at the same time. Some of it enjoyable, some of it not. I was still having periodic surgeries. Ida was still violent and unpredictable. She smashed the model cars that I had spent so much time building.

Hanging out with Jan was the only thing that kept me happy. She was a good listener, and I shared in her problems too. I knew how to make her laugh, and she knew how to make me laugh too. I loved her so much!

CHAPTER 6

THE CAMARO

One day I saw a 71 SS Camaro for sale at Fairfax Circle. I immediately knew I had to have this car! It was painted in custom colors and had several high- performance modifications. I had recently gotten my driver's license and I had about $1000 in the bank from working. Somehow, I talked my dad into cosigning a loan for $1800. When we picked up the car, my dad drove it home. He crunched my dual exhaust pipes on a speed bump, and he thought the transmission had a problem because it squealed the tires when it shifted gears. I didn't tell him it had a high- performance shift kit.

I was on top of the world! I had the baddest hot rod in my town, and the most beautiful girlfriend in the world! I took Jan for rides around town, and everybody would stare at my car. Once I jumped it off a hill and she hit her head on the top of the roof. She must've thought I was crazy, but I was just showing off again. We were indestructible teenagers.

When Jan couldn't hang out, I rode around with my sidekick, spark plug. On the first day of my junior year of high school, I got challenged to a drag race. A guy named Steve had a 71-Dodge Demon. It had a 340 engine and a few modifications. I think his buddy Mike egged him on to race me. I told him to bring it on. At lunchtime, we left school and headed out to route 66. Steve had Mike riding with him, and I had spark plug. We took off from a 10 mph roll and I beat him by about 2 feet. We were flying, and I was amazed that he even kept up with me. When I hit second gear, I jumped ahead 2 feet, and we stayed that way all the way to 140 mph. He wanted a rematch, and it turned out the same as the first race. We all went back to the school, and I was thrilled to be the fastest guy in the high school. Me and spark plug would cruise the parking lots of the other high schools, looking for a race. We found one at Springfield high school. It was a 69 Chevelle that looked pretty fast. We told him to meet us at our favorite drag racing spot, Fairfax Farms. We called it the farms. It was a stretch of route 50 just out of town. There was a parallel access road next to it where everybody parked.

We set the big race up for Friday night, and word went around both schools. When I showed up in my Camaro, there were about 100 people parked along the road to watch. I drank a few beers with my friends and waited for the Chevelle. He pulled in with racing slicks on his car. I told him that wasn't in the deal, and I uncapped my headers to even the odds. He agreed to that, and I swung my collectors around to open the exhaust. I did a practice run down the access road. This was partly to intimidate the competition, and partly to show off.

We both pulled out onto Route 50 and we had a flashlight start. His slicks gave him more traction off the line, and he jumped ahead of me. I was spinning my tires, and my car was a little sideways. Once my tires hooked up, I was gaining on him fast. My shift kit hit second gear and I spun my tires again. We were running neck and neck until about 100 mph when I shifted into third and went around him. The finish line was the two Washington signs on either side of the road. I hit my back up light switch as a sign of victory.

Instead of going straight to the turnaround, he got in the left lane and took the Washington exit. He took off without paying me. I went back to the party on the access road and celebrated my victory. It was a great race!

I had gone from being a nobody, to a popular guy in school. On one hand, this may have been good for my social anxiety and low self-esteem. On the other hand, it may have gone to my head a little. Looking back, I probably wasn't spending enough time with Jan. She was the best thing in my life and I was being distracted by school, work, my car, new friends, and worst of all, drugs and alcohol. On top of all that the home life was terrible with Ida acting up and my dad drinking every night.

One day, I went to see Jan and she told me that I spent more time with my car than her. She gave me a final poem that ripped my heart apart. It had a reference to a Barbra Streisand song "the way we were." It said she wanted to break up and that we should just remember the good times. I thought all the good times were just beginning.

CHAPTER 7

DOWNWARD SPIRAL

I guess I took her for granted, and thought she loved me enough to always be there for me. I suspected that she liked another guy that was on the football team. Anyway, I was beyond devastated, and I went off the deep end. The drug and alcohol use got much worse, and I was suicidal. I didn't realize what I had till it was gone. I self-medicated the pain with more and more drugs and alcohol. I think I'm overly sensitive and this was an emotional pain that I had never felt before.

Things at work were going badly too. Somebody was stealing money, and the drawer was coming up short every day. Andy fired one person at a time, but the shortages continued. I think I was fourth to be fired. It didn't help matters that Andy's son, Scott, had gotten me in trouble. I was working with Scott on a Sunday, and it was just me and him. He said, "hey, let's smoke a bowl." I thought it was pot, but it was laced with PCP. I found myself in another world completely! When two cars pulled in for gas, I was just trying to function. Scott waited on one car, and I waited on the other. When we went to put the gas caps back on, we got the caps reversed. It took us forever to figure out why the gas caps wouldn't go back on. Then I was in the shop, just wishing I could think again, and a customer came in saying something. I couldn't even understand what he was saying, and all I could think of was to say, "we're all out of those." We probably had some complaints to the boss about that day. Anyway,

I was laid off, and the guy who was taking the money had six kids, and I wasn't a tattletale.

Things at home were getting worse. Ida's schizophrenia was turning violent. She called the cops on me, and I reacted out of pent-up anger, and I ripped the phone off the wall. When the cops arrived, it was Officer Poe. He knew me and my car. He was a good guy and he said, "what's going on here Bobby?" I explained the situation and told him I would leave the house. I left and got in my Camaro. I went 175 miles to my old neighborhood in New Jersey. There's something therapeutic about driving 100 miles, like the James Taylor song.

In New Jersey I found a few friends and I drag raced for money. There was a Baldwin Motion Camaro that I beat for $50. Gas was $.40 a gallon, so that bought a lot of gas.

There was a body shop that paid me just to park my car in front of their business. It was a sharp-looking paint job. The base color was Mulsanne blue, and it had progressively smaller panels of gold and purple on it.

I spent about a week and a half in New Jersey until I got a message from a friend that my sister Tami was worried about me and had called looking for me. Tami and I were very close, and somehow, she knew I was in New Jersey. I came back to VA and she said I could split her apartment with her. She had gotten away from our parents a year earlier. Now I was out too, and I felt bad for my other sister, Sandy, who was still at home with the parents.

Free at last! I was 16 and had my own apartment and a car! Tami and I both partied, and she had some drug using friends. Her friend Ernie always had some new drug to try. One day he had some "white cross" speed and gave me a few. He took a few, and we were so pumped up, we did a major overhaul on Jimmy Cassel's GTO. Jimmy was Tami's boyfriend. He had a red '68 GTO convertible. He lived two doors down from Ernie.

When we went to Ernie's house, we would say hi to his parents, and then climb the fold down ladder up to his attic. Ernie was a home remodeler, and a carpenter. His attic was the ultimate hippy pad. He would put a record on the turntable and break out the tokemaster. For those who never used a tokemaster, it's a water filled bong. We would climb down the ladder and say goodbye to his parents. They didn't seem to have a clue. One day me, Ernie and my sister went up to the attic and they were shooting cocaine. They told me to try it, but I wasn't ready for that yet, and I said no thanks.

About 10 of my friends had hot rods, and I seemed to be a mechanic for all of them. Many of them had been bought by their parents. Living in the suburb of Washington DC, there were a lot of government and military families. Most families were upper class and the kids my age usually had money. This created a lot of partying and a lot of drugs. Every night there would be at least one house party at someone's house. Mostly, we had our outside party places, like the railroad tracks, Clarks Landing, and a lot of our secret secluded spots. Sometimes the cops chased us out.

I was still hurting emotionally from the breakup with Jan. I missed having someone that I could talk to, that understood. She had been through her struggles too. I didn't care about myself much, and I took deadly risks. There was a country road with a rise and a drop off to it. I took it at 50 mph. Then I tried it at 60, and then 70. At 70, my Camaro would come off the ground about 2 feet. A couple days later, I had a few friends riding with me and I hit a bump at about 75 mph.

I banged third gear as I crested the hill. The motor revved as I left the ground and I landed on my back wheels with a screech of tires. I rode a wheelie for about 30 yards and landed it perfectly. My friends were freaked out, and we all had a case of "beer nuts". That's when your beer overflows in your crotch.

Another stunt that I pulled was when I ran into three of my friends and they were tripping on LSD. They were two girls and a guy, and they said let's take a ride in your car. I had just changed the rear end gear ratio to a 3.08 and I decided to check my top speed on route 66. I got a lot of my kicks on route 66, as they say in the song. Anyway, I got on the highway and gradually increased my speed from 55 to 65, and 75, 85, 95. The three passengers were freaking out. At 105 I shifted into high gear. I went faster and faster till my speedometer was buried at 160. At that point I was passing cars that were going 55 like some kind of video game. I could've gone faster, but I was getting some vibration and it was even starting to freak me out. I slowed it back down and took them back to their house. I may have traumatized one or two of them. They talked about that one for years. Looking back, I shouldn't have put my friends at risk.

I continued to drag race at the farms on the weekends and it was the highlight of my week. I only lost once when I snapped a U joint on my driveshaft. I used an 11/16 socket in place of a U joint cap, so I could drive my car home.

I got a new job at Firestone tire company at Picket shopping center. I learned front end alignment from the mechanic, Joe. He was a good guy and a good teacher. They had me doing mechanic work, but I was getting tire changer pay. The boss would buy beer at the 7-Eleven after work, even though I was underage. We would all drink beer after work, and I think that only contributed to my alcoholism. I made a good friend there named Donnie. He was your typical hippie, with hair down to his waistline, and he always looked high. He was a very mellow person, and he would give me bong hits out in his car. He reminded me of Cheech, from Cheech and Chong. He had a party at his house one night, and there was a bunch of people there. I was still very shy around people and my social anxiety was bad. We were playing a game of quarters, where you bounce a quarter into the other person's glass, and they have to drink the whole glass. I was losing the game, but I was winning my battles with social anxiety. I remember thinking, wow, alcohol is the cure for my shyness! This would be a long, painful decision to self-medicate with alcohol. Any social situation required alcohol now.

In school, there was a program called ICT. It had something to do with career training. They allowed you to leave school early if you were going to work. My ICT teacher was Mr. Turner. He was a great guy and a great teacher. In one of his classes, I won the spelling bee with the word "rhetoric". My friend won "most money made". I won "most hours worked". All the "cool" kids hung out in the smoking area behind the school. We would do bleach burnouts with our cars. The disciplinarian of our school was Mr. Manning. He asked me to fix a couple things on his car. He had a big block Chrysler, and I test drove it to the back of the school, where I couldn't resist the urge to smoke the tires. I had it running great, and it smoked a mean tire. All my friends were laughing. Somehow, I got away with that one, and Mr. Manning complimented me on how good his car was running.

Another day, I was at the smoking area between classes, and a bunch of Fairfax cops grabbed me and handcuffed me. They threw me in a cop car and asked for identification. They thought I was an escaped convict!. Once they figured out the mistake, they let me go. I was late for my next class, and the teacher had a hard time believing my story. My friends from the smoking area were asking me, "What did you do?" I explained how things like that only happen to me, and they happen all the time.

On days when I didn't have to work, my friend, Tommy and I would drop a hit of acid before our last class started. At the end of class, we would be starting to get off. We would glance across at each other laughing. Then it was game on. We would cruise in our hot rods with Skynyrd playing in the 8-track player. We drank beer like it was water when we were tripping. Tami worked as a bank teller, and one time I was riding around with my friends, and I pulled into the drive-through. She sent me out a bag of weed through the drive-through! My friends thought that was the coolest thing ever.

I returned the favor to Tami and her boyfriend, Jimmy by stocking the apartment with beer. One of my friends, Steve and I, were kind of juvenile delinquents. I guess we all were. He told us there was a box car full of beer on the railroad tracks. Me and a couple of friends went down there and filled our cars to the max. We pulled out of there like we all were driving low riders. We carried 54 cases up to my third-floor apartment in the middle of the night and stacked them in an empty closet. Then I filled the fridge completely full. When Jimmy and Tami got up in the morning, they had quite a sight when they open the fridge! Then I said "open the closet" and they saw cases of beer from the floor to the ceiling! That was quite a night of mischief.

After we carried all the beer up the stairs, we were starving. We were headed to 7- Eleven at four in the morning and we saw the bread guy dropping off pallets of donuts at the rear loading dock at the grocery store. After he left, we scored about 20 boxes of donuts. There's nothing like a dozen donuts and a couple of six packs of low quality beer to make you puke your guts out. Another epic night!

I was building a racing motor for my Camaro up in the apartment. It's a good thing Tami was so cool about it. When the short block was complete, we carried it down the stairs and installed it in the Camaro. The manager of the apartment building was bitching about us working on the car in the parking lot. I got permission for one day of work, and I had the heads on, and the car running in one day. They were probably worried about liability because Tami's Camaro had fallen off the bumper jack onto me. I wasn't hurt, but I was pinned under it, and somebody finally walked by and jacked up the car for me.

I had a brief fling with a girl named Laura when I lived at the apartment. I had a hard time telling her that I still loved Jan. I was a confused young man. My friend Mark and I were at Laura's apartment drinking beer one night and Mark was pretty trashed. We left there in his 67 Camaro, and he was showing off for his girlfriend I guess, burning his tires and flying through the apartment complex. He lost control and hit a telephone pole at about 50 miles an hour. I had just had a surgery on my nose and I still had the bandages on. My nose got re-broken, and my face broke the windshield. Mark lost a couple of teeth on the steering wheel, I think. Our girlfriends came running to the car, and I remember telling them to get the beer out of the car before the cops got there. We both got ambulance rides to the emergency room. My nose has been crooked ever since. My dad took me to the plastic surgeon, and he said it had healed crooked. That was a really hard hit. The telephone pole didn't break, and the car was totaled.

I was still working at Firestone, and every paycheck either went to buy high- performance parts for the Camaro, or to drugs and alcohol. I don't know which addiction was worse, the car, or the drugs and alcohol. I would also do side jobs on my friend's cars to pay for my habits.

I met a whole new group of friends while working and hanging around Picket shopping center. Two of these were Steve Wilkinson and Donnie Tobin. Steve was one of a kind. He was a tall guy, and he always carried a guitar around with him. He could really play the guitar! He got me started playing and showed me a lot of stuff. I bought a red Epiphone electric guitar with a little amp and a fuzz box. I would practice for hours. I wasn't one of those "naturals" that learn guitar quick. I have big hands and fat fingers. I had to really work at it. Steve would show me how to play some Skynyrd songs, and I would practice till I got them halfway down pat. Then I would ask him to show me some other stuff.

Steve took flying lessons and eventually got a pilot's license. One day we went to Dulles Airport and rented a Cessna for a couple of hours. The plane had dual controls, and he let me fly and land a couple of times. I had a blast! I also learned a new skill.

And in exchange, he wanted to drag race my Camaro. We went to McLaren Road next to Redskin Park, and I let him race it down the road. His girlfriend rode with him, and I think it scared her a little because he cooked my brakes getting it stopped at the end of the road.

Steve and I had some wild things happen, and we were probably a bad influence on each other. I guess the wildest thing was when we were cruising in my Camaro with our friend Leslie. We were parked in Centreville, VA, and she pulled out her cocaine and a needle. I guess I caved to peer pressure. Deep down, I knew I shouldn't do this. They both did theirs, and then Leslie gave me my first shot of cocaine. My first immediate sensation was the taste of the drug. It was the same taste as all my surgeries, where they packed my nostrils with long gauze strips, treated with pharmaceutical cocaine. Then my ears were buzzing with a very strange sound. I got a feeling of euphoria like I never had before. The first time was a scary experience. I got the feeling I had crossed a line that I could never return from. After about five minutes I felt like I could function again. We left there and headed back towards Fairfax on route 29–211. I was still very high, and I wound the Camaro up to about 120 mph. As I crested a hill, I could see a Mercedes pulling onto the road in front of me. I locked up my brakes and skidded about 50 yards straight towards the Mercedes. My car was a little sideways and I let off my brake pedal right before I hit him. This made my car shoot to the left and I missed him by a couple of feet. My car jumped a curb on the left side of the highway and bent my left front wheel bad. I was in the grass medium strip, and I maneuvered my way back onto the high-way, basically going around the Mercedes. This whole scary event took about 15 seconds, but it felt like a lifetime. I remember Leslie screaming and bracing herself to the dashboard. I limped my car to the closest party spot and got some friends to help me go get another wheel. That was a close one! If I would've hit that Mercedes, we could all be dead.

I remember feeling terrible when I came down from the cocaine and drinking a lot of beer to calm my nerves. This period was when the good times of partying became bad times. The drugs made me want to drink, and drinking impaired my judgment and made me want drugs. It was becoming a vicious cycle. Not only for me, but for most of my friends. Leslie liked to smoke PCP, and she had a boyfriend who smoked it too. I was sleeping on her couch one night, and he came in about two in the morning. He went upstairs and shot her in the neck with a 22. He walked right past me, and I don't think he realized I was there. He was out of his mind on PCP. It's a drug that distorts reality so much that people do crazy things. If he realized I was there, I'm sure he would've shot me too. He was later arrested at the nearby 7-Eleven, and Leslie was taken to the hospital. I visited her there and she was paralyzed from the neck down. It was heartbreaking to see such a beautiful girl in that condition. She was a good friend, and I would visit her a lot. Even after she came home to her parents' house. I came to see her, and I met her parents.

After a month or so of being home, she got permission to go out to a club with me. I really liked her, and I didn't care about her condition. I would have been willing to take care of her, but she didn't feel the same way about me. I wheeled her to my truck and lifted her into the seat. We went to a club that had a band playing. After a couple drinks, she ran into one of her old friends. They were outside and smoking some PCP. I couldn't believe she did that after all she's been through. She told me they would take her home and I left there completely disgusted. I never hung out with Leslie again. Meanwhile, working at Firestone in the Picket Shopping Center, Donnie , and a few other guys decided to steal a case of beer from the 7-Eleven. There was an opening in the corner of Pickett shopping center, and we were partying in the woods behind there. One guy distracted the cashier, while another guy went in the cooler and grabbed the beer. He ran out of the store with two cases of beer, lunch, meat, bread, and a few other things stacked on the beer up to his chin. The cashier went to chase him, but we were all standing around and blocking his way. We all met up later behind the shopping center.

We were all having a good old time, drinking beer, and eating sandwiches in the woods behind the shopping center. As I was looking around, I saw cop cars surrounding us. I warned everybody and then I found a good tree to climb. I never climbed a tree so fast, as I went all the way up to the top. I could see the flashlights shining all around. I kept perfectly still, and lights were even shining up into the trees. I went all the way up to the top. They caught everyone but me, and I had to stay up in the tree for at least an hour. About a month later, we were hanging out in the parking lot in front of 7-Eleven. There was me, spark plug, and our friend Tracy. A couple of bikers pulled in and bumped into the car in front of them. Tracy was laughing at them as I went into 7-Eleven to get a couple beers. When I came out, the first thing I saw was the biggest biker arguing with Tracy. He drew back his fist like he was about to hit her. I set my beers down and ran at him at full speed. He didn't see me coming at him from the side. I hit him hard and knocked him down in the parking lot. I was on top of him, and he was trying to get his breath back. I had knocked the wind out of him. I remember hearing someone say, "look out Bobby!" The next thing I knew, the other biker punched me hard in my forehead. I got up off the first guy, and he was holding his hand in pain.

He had broken his hand on my hard head. Both bikers got in their car and drove away. I threw a full beer at their car as they left. I had a cut above my eye. About an hour later, a whole gang of bikers pulled in and wanted revenge. Apparently, both of their friends were in the hospital. There was a girl waving a broken bottle, and about 15 others. I was thinking this could be big trouble. They were asking where the guy was who beat up their friends, but nobody was talking. They didn't know who to fight so they finally left. If they were a little smarter, they would've known it was the guy with the cut above his eye.

My sister, Tami and I went to a lot of concerts together. She would always give me a ticket. Ernie and her boyfriend, Jimmy, would come along with a few others. We saw Fleetwood Mac, Rod Stewart, Led Zeppelin, ZZ Top, The Outlaws, Blue Öyster Cult, Little Feat, the Doobie Brothers, and a few others like The Who.

Ernie was into all kinds of music, and he talked us into going to a bluegrass concert in Galax, VA. It was a fun ride down, with all of us riding in the van, drinking beer and smoking pot. When we got there, it was a great festival with thousands of people. The stage was in a valley, and the audience sat on the hillsides. I had a cold and a cough, and I was drinking cough syrup to help it. Then it began to rain, but the bands kept playing. There were three or four dirt paths going down to the stage, and they all turned to mud. As I was walking down one of these paths towards where my sister was sitting, I found myself sliding on my bare feet. Next thing I know I am mud surfing at about 40 mph! I hit a hump in the path and went flying through the air. I landed back on my feet still mud surfing. The ground leveled out and I slammed into the stage at about 50 mph! I remember the sound of thousands of people cheering and hooting and hollering. I went to walk back up the hill and I slipped and fell flat on my face in the mud. Then I heard thousands of people laughing.

A lot of other people tried to mud surf the hill, but nobody stayed upright. I made it to where Tammy and my friends were sitting, and they were all laughing hysterically. We watched as people tried to repeat my stunt and failed. It was epic!

Tami's boyfriend, Jimmy, had a 68 GTO that was fast, and we went to Old Dominion Speedway in Manassas, VA. one weekend. I had done a lot of the work on his car, and I couldn't believe it when he threw me the keys and told me to go race it. I did a couple runs and qualified in a bracket with similar cars. I won a couple of races until I went too fast for my bracket, and lost. It was a lot of fun though. The use of PCP was causing many of my friends to change into walking zombies. Jimmy turned into one of these people. It was so sad. Tami ended their relationship eventually. He was devastated, which made him get worse. I never enjoyed the high of PCP, and I'm glad Tami didn't either. The aftereffects were having trouble thinking, and I'm sure it caused brain damage. In our area, it was called "Killer weed" or KW. Some people called it "green". It would be sold in film tins. A "tin of green" would be $30-$40. Sometimes it would be pot treated with PCP. This was called "love boat".

When I was in my senior year of high school, I had my last surgery, and my dad took me to a specialist in Pittsburgh. I heard him explain to the doctor about how he believed the nuclear testing had caused Sandy and me to be born with birth defects. The doctor reviewed all of my unsuccessful surgeries to repair the roof of my mouth, the cleft palate, and suggested a retainer that would cover the roof of my mouth. I wish they had done this about 10 years earlier. I can speak almost normal now. The surgery on my nose and upper lip kept me out of school for a week, and towards the end of my senior year, I was suspended from school for missing too many days. My teacher, Mr. Turner, got me back in school by persuading most of my teachers to let me make up my schoolwork. My English teacher refused, and I had to go to summer school to graduate. At the end of the summer, there was a graduation party at a nearby park and I borrowed my friend's 63 Corvette, and did a burnout in front of Mr. Turner. Mr. Turner was a very cool teacher. He taught gym, drivers Ed, and ICT. I thought the burnout was funny. Anyway, high school was over! Hallelujah!

Life at Firestone was getting dull. Donnie and I would do bong hits in the Alley parking lot, and then have a race to see who could mount and balance 4 tires and mount them on a car the fastest. We both won a couple times, taking about five minutes. I think it was a mutual agreement between me and the boss when I left there. I told all my friends "I worked at Firestone, but I got fired for getting stoned!"

CHAPTER 8

TRUCK DRIVIN' MAN

It didn't take long to find a better job. I got hired at A+A Transfer Co. It was a small company owned by two men, Dick and Bob. Cliff was Dick's son, and he was the driver. I started as a laborer and mechanic. They had two trucks; both were F600 Fords. One was a flatbed, and one was a box truck. They were both a faded army green color. The flatbed we called the cable truck because we hauled reels of heavy copper cable on that one. At first, we did all our work for C+P telephone. That stood for Chesapeake and Potomac. We hauled everything from office furniture to the concrete pads that were under a telephone booth.

Cliff was quite a character. He liked to smoke his green, and I was sometimes afraid to ride with him. He would pull up alongside a pedestrian and act like he was pointing a gun at them. Then he would turn the ignition key off and then back on creating a backfire from the muffler. This would scare the hell out of the pedestrian, and they would usually fall to the ground.

Cliff would laugh hysterically. The boss wondered why I had to replace the muffler so often, but I didn't tell. Often times Cliff would throw fresh fruit at people. One morning, he loaded four or five concrete pads at the very back end of the box truck. We were exiting 495 onto Route one, and the truck was so heavy in the back that it didn't turn right to make the exit. We hit barrels full of Liquid that were there as safety barriers. I bounced around in the cab, but I wasn't hurt.

We pulled over, and the left front fender was smashed in. We were lucky the truck was still right side up. A few months after this, Cliff's dad passed away. Now, the company was owned by Bob. Cliff saw a fertilizer sign one day that said "green power" and he tied it to the front of the truck. Then he drove by his friend's house to show it off.

Another day, in Arlington, he stopped at a used car lot and test drove a Ford Fairlane. I was riding along, and it was like a scene out of The Blues Brothers.

He burned rubber out of the lot, went sideways around a few corners, and then pulled back into the lot. "I'll take it!" he said. The salesman was white as a ghost. He drove the car home and I drove the truck.

Cliff and I had a mutual friend named Eddie. Eddie and all of us were at a party one night and the cops came to break it up. I witnessed a cop slamming his head in the parking lot, and Eddie never moved after that. A lot of people witnessed this. The cop threw him in the car and took him to jail.

We found out the next day that Eddie had died. The cops claimed that he hung himself, but I know from experience that they take your shoelaces, your belt, and any other means of hanging yourself. They apparently covered up a murder.

Cliff and two of his friends blew up this cop's car and got caught. I believe they each did three years in prison. A famous guitarist, Roy Buchanan, also supposedly hung himself in the Fairfax jail on August 14, 1988. The death was described as suspicious. With Cliff gone from A+A, I was the only driver for a while. I loved the job because I loved to drive.

I thought about Jan almost every day. I was still hurting from the breakup and I soothed the pain with drugs and alcohol. I was good at keeping work and partying separate. I met a few girls, but I was so socially awkward that nothing worked.

There was a park by my house, called Van Dyke Park, where everybody hung out. It had a big parking lot, and we would throw frisbees, drink beer, and smoke pot. We had some good times there, and a lot of nice cars would cruise in and out. I was cruising through downtown Fairfax city one night in the Camaro, and I came to a red light in front of the Huddleston library on University Drive. As I sat there, waiting for the light, a bunch of partiers were in the front of the library, egging me on saying "come on dude, light em up!" Since I was sitting on an uphill slope, I knew I could pull off a good burn out. The light turned green, and I popped the clutch in first gear at about 4000 RPM. My car just sat there smoking the tires, until the whole crowd was in a cloud of smoke. As I reached the intersection and turned left, I saw a cop car to my right. I quickly let off the gas, but it was too late. The flashing red lights came on and I pulled over. The cop put me in the backseat of his car, and I was thinking my goose was cooked. The partiers from the library were walking past me, sitting in the cop car, and laughing at me. The cop gave me the third degree, and then he said "you're lucky boy, if I was a city cop, I would impound your car and take you to jail, but I'm a county cop, so I have to let you go". Damn! That was another close call! I got in my car and waited till the cop left. Then I made two left turns and came back to the same light. I looked around the corner to my right this time, and then I smoked those people out even worse. Then I went to Van Dyke Park and had a few beers to calm my nerves. I think my next paycheck went towards a new set of back tires.

CHAPTER 9

CHRISTINE

I met a girl around this time that hung out at Van Dyke Park. I'm not going to use her real name, because I don't have a lot of good things to say about her. I'm going to call her Christine, after the car movie. In that movie, the main character had an unhealthy addiction to a car that had demons. I had an unhealthy attraction to a girl with her demons.

It started with her following me around like my shadow. She asked me if she could ride with me, and I was too nice to say no. She was attractive, but maybe a little bit annoying. She would seek attention by talking about her problems, and she would laugh after every sentence. She told me her brother and her father abused her, but I found out that wasn't true. She was a compulsive liar and had a hard time telling the truth. On the other hand, it was nice to have someone around, and we ended up as boyfriend and girlfriend. It was the start of a toxic relationship. She was a small girl, about 5 feet tall, with long brown hair. She was slim and attractive. We had our share of adventures, I guess.

One winter night, I was driving her Opel Kadett on route 123 towards Burke lake. The speed limit was about 45 mph. I was doing about 55, and I came around the bend to see water spraying across the road. Some idiot had opened a fire hydrant, and a powerful stream of water hit the side of the car. An Opel Kadett is a very small, very light car. The water knocked the car sideways, and I was sliding on ice.

The water had frozen to the road. Several cars were spun out all along the roadside. I drifted the Opel like some kind of dirt track racer, and finally got it straight. I pulled over to help anyone that might be hurt. There was a Mercedes that was flipped up on its side, and a young guy, and a girl were trapped inside. I jumped up on the top of the car and tried to pull the door open. It was really heavy with the car on its side like that. I finally got it open, and they climbed out. The girl was hysterical. Everyone else seemed to be OK. I found some flares, and I had to cross back through the powerful stream of water to put them out along the road. The kids thanked me for getting them out, and I went along my way.

Meanwhile, Tami went to Alaska to work on the Alaskan pipeline. I felt kind of abandoned, still in VA, and I missed her a lot. I briefly shared an apartment with my younger sister, Sandy, and she had her first baby, Amanda, while we lived there.

I had a friend named Ricky, who was almost as crazy as me. The first time I met him in high school, he rolled is VW bug onto its roof in the high school parking area. I remember how funny the bug looked upside down and spinning around. Whenever I rolled the bug that I had, I would just buckle up, and I always managed to land it back onto its wheels. Ricky and I rode into DC a few times, and he introduced me to a strip joint in D.C. called "Good Guys". One night, we came out of there, half liquored up, and started rat racing through downtown DC. I have no idea how we got away with that. We were burning rubber and going sideways around corners. Mostly, I was following him because I would've gotten lost! He had a nice gold colored GTO. We turned the capital of our fine country into our own personal Nascar track.

I had another incident that involved Rickey. We had been out at a friend's party in the country. At the party, I smoked some PCP, and my judgment was extremely impaired. When I coupled that with alcohol, it was a recipe for disaster. I left the party with Ricky behind me, and I opened it up when I hit Braddock Road. My judgment of speed was way off, and I was going way faster than I thought I was. I came around a slight bend, and the road was slightly wet. The Camaro slid off the right side of the road into the ditch. There was a row of mailboxes, mounted to a 4 x 4, and I took out the whole thing. The 4 x 4 came through my windshield and went right between the two front bucket seats. The mailboxes sounded like machine guns as they deflected off my windshield. I was sliding sideways through someone's front yard. There was a huge tree in the middle of their front yard. As if by divine intervention, my car spun around 180°, and missed the tree. I finally came to a stop with my back wheels in the ditch and my front wheels hanging out into the road.

I crawled out of the car and took the return spring off of my carburetor. The Camaro had a tunnelram intake, and a Holley carb sticking out of the hood. I took the return spring off, so I would have something to blame the wreck on. As I looked around, there were mailboxes everywhere, my skid marks seemed to go around the big tree, and my Camaro was a mess! It had a 6 foot long 4 x 4, sticking out of the windshield. It would have impaled me if it had been 8 inches to the left. About that time, Ricky came pulling up and everybody jumped out of his car to see if I was OK. The only thing wrong with me was drugs and alcohol. They took me to the hospital in an ambulance to check me over. I repaired the Camaro, but the custom paint job was ruined. The Camaro took another hit when a young girl ran a red light and smashed my right front fender.

The next hit was when I was in Reston, VA and I slid on some ice. I hit a huge tree head on, and it bent the frame. I limped it home with the front tires squealing from being so crooked, and parked it in my parent's backyard. I parked it under the tree that I had used to change the engine six times. I could just kick myself in the ass for the bad decisions I made, and for tearing up my Camaro.

I started riding with Christine in her Opel Kadett, and we were both pretty much homeless for quite a while. I took out the divider between the backseat and the trunk. That way we could both stretch out and sleep in the car at night. We had a dog too, named Tasha. Tasha was a shepherd husky mix that was part coyote. She was a great watchdog too. If anyone came anywhere near the car, she would bark. I would unplug the ignition switch under the dash in case a cop came around. I would say the car wouldn't start. This happened once, and I turned the key for him, and nothing happened. I showed him my mechanic hands and said I would fix it myself. After he left, I would plug in the switch and drive to a better spot.

I was building a 68 old's 442 at the time. I totally rebuilt a 455 cubic inch engine from a Toronado. The car finally got done. I was working every day at A+A Transfer Co., and on the weekends, it would be party time.

I would get two paychecks a week. One for driving the trucks, and one for my hours working on them. I would buy some cocaine and beer. Then I would buy more coke and beer. And then more and more, until I was broke. Coming down from coke would give me an overwhelming urge for more. On Monday morning, I would be drained and broke, but it would be time to move a four-bedroom house. The small company had grown into a moving company also. I would tell myself every Monday, "I'll never do that again", but every Friday I would do it again. Christine was also into the same drugs plus LSD. At that point, I had experimented with pot, alcohol, cocaine, mescaline, nebutol, Hash, LSD, Quaaludes, PCP, opioids, speed, and other drugs. I don't think I cared much about myself, and I was self-medicating the pain of losing Jan, and all of my other problems. My philosophy was, I'm not dealing drugs, and I'm not hurting anyone, so I'll do whatever I want to.

There was a party one night at a friend's house, and I walked about 5 miles to it in the snow. Christine's brother John was there. He was pretty drunk, and he was trying to start a fight with me. He said Christine had told him that I threatened her with a shotgun. I told him that wasn't true, and that she had told me that he had beaten her. To avoid a fight, I left and walked 5 miles back home.

I devised to plan to catch her lying. I hooked up a tape recorder to my phone and I gave her a call. I told her I'd run into her brother at the party, and he accused me of threatening her. She proceeded to say I had never threatened her. I even went into greater detail about threatening her with a gun. She once again denied that I had ever threatened her. Then I went to see her brother. He was sober and I played the tape for him. We agreed that she had lied to both of us, and we resolved this issue. John died from a heart attack a week later. If I would've have fought him, I could've killed him. Christine's lies were proving to be quite dangerous.

Working for the moving company was interesting, and after getting over the weekend, it would be almost fun sometimes. It was hard work, but it was great for burning the chemicals out of my system. We met a lot of interesting people, and some would tip us after the job was done. I noticed that the poor people were better tippers than the wealthy people.

Some of our more memorable jobs were moving a load of Chinese computers through DC to a convention center. We had to do it when traffic was the lightest because they were very fragile. Then we moved one of Jimmy Carter's family members into a pair of adjoining town houses in Arlington. We moved the whole Iranian embassy out of DC, while they had 50 American hostages. I believe they stiffed my boss on their bill. We also moved several of the Redskins football players. We went from two old trucks to a brand new 77 GMC 6500 series then another 6500, and then we added truck after truck. The boss hired a lot of new workers and I was appointed to a new contract hauling phones for western electric. I would use the box truck and pick up about 12 pallets of phone supplies going to about six stops around Arlington, VA. Every day I stopped at the Pentagon, the Navy Annex, department of defense, Arlington Hall, and the CIA in McLean. This was before terrorists, and nobody would even check me or the truck. I would roll pallets of new phones in and take the defective ones out. They would go back to the western electric factory. They were rotary and pushbutton phones.

Occasionally, somebody would pull out in front of me, and I would have to slam the brakes on. I remember the sound of thousands of phones ringing when all the pallets tipped over. I would have to sort everything back out. I would eat lunch at the Navy annex. They had great food, and I was the only long-haired hippy in the midst of a lot of crewcut military guys. I got a lot of strange looks.

I had a very rough two weeks during this period. It started one day on this route. I picked up three or four huge switching racks. They were about 6 feet tall and weighed a ton. The boss was with me that day to lend a hand. They loaded the racks onto the truck with a forklift. When I got to the Western electric factory to unload them, we decided to lay them down onto pallets. When we were tipping the first one, it slid into the second, and the third, and they all came down on us. It was like dominoes that weighed a ton each. My boss had his arm pinned against the side of the truck, and I must've gotten a rush of adrenaline because I lifted them long enough for him to get his arm out. I remember him asking me if I was on drugs. He couldn't believe I lifted them.

Later in the day, I realized that my back was seriously hurting. I went to the doctor, and they prescribed me opiates to relieve the pain. The opiates made me drowsy and caused me to have another accident. I was putting antifreeze in my radiator and my fingers went into the fan of my car. It sliced my fingers up badly. It was a sharp aluminum racing fan. I had to go to the hospital and get my finger stitched up. They gave me more opiates.

The next day I went to a party in the country west of Fairfax. It was a huge party, and my friend Joe was playing there with his band "Six Shooter". We were all having a good time, and I was sitting in my car doing some coke and smoking weed with a few friends, when a fight broke out. It was a young local guy fighting with a friend of mine. He was way outnumbered, and I guess he decided to go home and get a couple rifles. He came back and hid in the woods, shooting at people that were standing around the party. I remember the sounds of two different guns, and I thought there were at least two shooters. A bullet whizzed passed me and shattered a car window directly behind me.

It must've missed me by about 6 inches. Everybody was running towards the house to find some cover. Another friend of mine was grazed by a bullet. Somebody called the cops, and they finally arrived.

After a while, they had a guy in custody. I didn't feel like sticking around because I thought there were two shooters. I got in my car and headed towards home. I was driving a cheap Camaro, since my good one was wrecked, and I got pulled over about a mile from the party. I had been drinking at the party, and the cop asked me to blow into a breathalyzer. I told him I had a cleft palate and couldn't blow up a balloon if I wanted to. The truth is, I could if I held my nose shut, but I didn't tell him that. He put me in his car and headed to the local hospital to get me a blood test. I bailed out of the car on the way at about 40 mph. I took off running through weeds and bushes. I heard him yell "stop! or I'll shoot!" I kept running. He never shot at me and never caught me. My plan was to escape long enough to sober up. A DWI would probably cost me my job plus a lot of money.

I slept in the woods that night, and I turned myself in in the morning. I registered a .09 blood alcohol content, which was barely under the limit of .10. They threw me in the Woodstock Virginia jail. The local guy who shot people was out the next day, but they left me in there for a week. They had taken away my pain meds, and I was hurting bad. My back was killing me, and my fingers were throbbing. I had to keep my left hand elevated. I was at Woodstock, but it wasn't the concert. It was the Woodstock, VA jail. One guy was drying banana peels and smoking them. He offered me a hit, but I had to pass.

A week later, I finally appeared before a judge. He asked the cop why I had been left in there for a week with no trial. The cop didn't have any good reasons. They wrote me up for a future court date and released me. I was taken to a towing yard where my car had been impounded to. I made arrangements to pay that bill and drove away. When I stopped at the first store, I checked everything in my car.

There was about a gram of cocaine in the glove box! I'm thinking, how the hell did that get there? It wasn't mine, though it was now.

I tasted it, and it wasn't too bad. Nothing special, but I took a big snort of it anyway. My first thought was that it was planted by the cops. Oh well, I'm free at last! Jail cells are enough to drive a free spirit insane! I drove the seventy mile trip east on route 66 back to Fairfax and my friends were so glad to see me. They thought I had been shot. I had to explain the whole incident to my boss, who wasn't very happy with me, and then it was back to work driving the trucks.

In the following months, I made a few trips to Woodstock for court dates, and I was required to attend ASAP classes (Alcohol Safety Action Program). I was charged with escape and DUI. The DUI wouldn't go on my record since I was .09, if I completed the program successfully. By escaping and sobering up a little, I had saved my driver's license and my job. The escape fine was $125 and well worth it. The ASAP program cost me $1800, and my lawyer was $1500. I believe it was about 18 weeks in the ASAP program. They asked me if I had ever thought about suicide, and I made the mistake of being honest. Then they sent me to a psychiatrist, who then agreed with me and sent me back to ASAP. During these classes, they taught me how to calculate my blood alcohol content (BAC), by calculating the number of drinks, or beers, the number of hours drinking, and my body weight. In other words, how to drink and drive successfully. I could smell alcohol in this classroom and even the teacher talked about her drinking on the weekends.

I finally completed ASAP successfully and had my final court date in Woodstock. They dropped the DUI and as I was walking out of the court room the cop handed me another warrant. This one was for felony cocaine possession. What the hell? He said they found a baggie with residue, and they sent it out for testing before they charged me. More trips to Woodstock for more court dates. I was beyond pissed. They were making a scapegoat of me, and a local kid who shot people got a slap on the wrist. I don't think I ever had any coke in my car to begin with. When I did coke, I didn't leave leftovers sitting around. I would do it until it was gone. I paid another 1500 to my lawyer and got a year's probation. The felony was dropped. All this stress and aggravation just fueled my drug use.

Back at work, the boss was buying new trucks left and right. I guess business was good for him. He bought a tractor and trailer, and I was top dog on the totem pole to drive it. It was an International with a caterpillar 3208 engine. The boss got a contract with World Airways to haul air mail from Dulles airport in VA, to BWI airport in MD. He had the 40-foot trailer painted with a 747 jet that was about 30 feet long. The tractor got a white paint job too, and the A+A lettering on the doors. I would pick up a trailer load of air mail at Dulles airport and take it to BWI in Baltimore every day. Driving a tractor trailer on the beltway around DC is probably the most stressful thing you could possibly do. I would pick up a 12 pack of beer on the way home to calm my nerves after work. I would never drink or do drugs at work except once on a moving job when we found a quarter ounce of coke under someone's couch cushion. I would turn off the service elevator in between floors and sneak a few snorts. I figured what could they do, call the police? What would they say? "hey, the mover stole my cocaine"? There were lots of stories from the moving days.

Meanwhile, Christine was dating a guy who followed the Grateful Dead. She would ride around with him in his step van. I was actually hurt by this, because I had become attached to her.

I found an old house right on Main Street. It was at the corner of Railroad and Main. There were two buildings. One was an apartment above a garage. The main house had four bedrooms, and the total rent per month was $150. The owner told me the house was scheduled for demolition in a year or so. I rented the apartment to my friend Bill. There were five people altogether and the rent was only $35 each. I only paid $10. Bill was heavy into drugs, as all of us were, I guess. I was the only one working. I usually ended up covering a few people who couldn't scrape up $35 for rent. One day, I looked out the front window and saw a beautiful blonde girl hitchhiking on Main Street. I ran out the back door and jumped into my car. I was spinning wheels to get out of my driveway, when I saw my friend Tommy and his Trans Am Firebird. I had to cut him off because he was trying to pick her up too. I managed to get there first and pick her up.

Her name was Holly, and she was a lifeguard at the pool down the street. She told me her boyfriend was in jail, and I asked her if she wanted to stay with me. She agreed and I slept with her that night. I was in love with her for about a week. Then came the day when I got home from work, and she was in my bed with my roommate Gary. Gary was a guy who was homeless, and I gave him a home. I was livid! Maybe I loved too deeply, and I expected the same in return. Anyway, I proceeded to tear the house to pieces. First, I slammed the front door so hard that the glass kept going out onto the porch. I kicked a few holes in the wall and ripped the stove and fridge out of the kitchen, smashing them. I told Gary and Holly to get the hell out. I started punching windows out. The house was about due for demolition anyway. As I punched out the kitchen window, the glass pinched my right arm as it was drawing back out of the window. I cut my wrist clear down to the bone. It went through the artery and the tendon. The next thing I knew I was shooting streams of blood out of my wrist with every heartbeat. There was blood all over the side of the house.

I grabbed my arm and squeezed it to stop the bleeding. My friend Tommy took me to the emergency room in his Trans Am Firebird. I was soaked in blood from my waist down. I remember them rushing me in and a woman doctor named Dr. Fox repaired the damage. She shut off the blood flow with a tourniquet and did a lot of stitching, inside and out. It really hurt when she let the blood flow back into my arm. I also had nerve damage, and I had to later have reconstructive surgery. I left there with my arm elevated, and my heart broken. It was the beginning of the end for the party house at Railroad and Main.

We would have a batch of MDA occasionally, and everyone would be tripping on that. Then it would be a batch of coke, and I would start by snorting it, but end up shooting it up. I remember bending the needle of my syringe, and throwing it in the crawlspace under the house. The following Friday I would crawl under the house to get it and straighten it out. I would rinse it with alcohol and use it again. Looking back this was disgusting but it's how addiction controlled me. Bill was up for three or four days on methamphetamine and ended up in a mental hospital in Staunton, Virginia. I visited him there and it was a sad experience.

And one of the renters was named Roy. The electric bill was in his name, and it was overdue. He owed me rent too. All his money had gone to drugs. I had a band come to play on a Saturday night and I handed him the electric bill while they were jamming. Shortly after that, they turned off the electricity. Every night was a party at Railroad and Main, but the party was over.

It was strange, how drugs and alcohol had turned good friends into enemies. There were a lot of drug deals gone bad. Friends would rip off friends to get high. Guys who were recently healthy young athletes on the football team were now junkies, weighing half what they used to. I knew a few beautiful young girls who are now mentally gone from PCP. For some reason, heroin was not prevalent in Fairfax yet, but it was in DC.

My one and only experience with heroin was in DC. I had a bad habit of getting coked up and hanging out in the alleys of DC. At the time, it was the murder capital of the world. I guess I liked the excitement of it, and there were girls everywhere. All along 14th and 15th St., prostitutes would walk up and down the street. I would park somewhere and walk around the whole block, checking out all the girls like a kid in a candy store. I would pick up my favorite of the bunch and go to a hotel room.

Sometimes I would return to the street and pick up one or two more. On one night, the prostitute had heroin. This was right before aids came out, luckily. We mixed my cocaine with her heroin, making a speedball. She injected me first, and I was immediately higher than I have ever been before. There was a cheap black, and white TV with Robin Trower on it, playing guitar. The TV turned into a color TV. I felt like vomiting, and I went into the bathroom. I remember enjoying vomiting! We never even had sex. I came out of the bathroom, and she was sitting there, motionless, with the needle hanging out of her arm. I eventually pulled it out and she woke up. I left there and was high for about eight hours. They say that heroin users chase that first high, but never get it. I'm glad I didn't come across heroin after that. I did come across Dilaudid, which is also an opioid, and injected that with another DC prostitute. We both fell asleep in a slightly wooded area. When I woke up the next morning, I was staring at the front of the White House! We passed out in Lafayette Park. The country was a lot more relaxed before terrorism. For a few months, my favorite thing to do on payday was to get a quarter ounce of coke, and a case of beer, and hang out on the streets of DC. There were a lot of wild things that happened, but I won't go into all of them.

I definitely won't forget the time I was checking out the hookers in D.C. and a bunch of black women came up to me, asking for a date. The next thing I knew they had their hands in all my pockets and a death grip on my crotch. I had to break free and I was slinging hookers out into the street left and right. I was in great physical shape, and the adrenaline was pumping. The only way out of this mess was to grab one of them and spin around, using her to knock all the other ones down. All the white hookers got a kick out of the whole spectacle. They knew me by name at this point. It all ended with hookers laying everywhere. They didn't get a dime because my money was in my cowboy boot. Everyone who has ever messed with me has ended up wishing they hadn't. It was insane how I got a thrill out of flirting with disaster. I just didn't care about myself.

In my several years of driving for A+A, I had many close calls with idiots on the highway, but I only remember one minor accident. I would always look in my mirrors and leave myself a way out of any situation. I was driving on 495, the beltway around DC, when the whole tractor-trailer took a hard left turn. I went across two lanes, and barely kept it off the center median. I thought something in my steering had broken. I pulled off on the right shoulder and inspected the truck. It had made a noise like a machine gun when it happened.

I didn't see anything wrong with the truck and I noticed a guy pulled over up ahead. I walked up to see if he needed help and he didn't know what had happened either. When I saw the circular scrapes on his left rear quarter panel, I figured out what happened. He was in my blind spot, and he had drifted over and hit my right front wheel. If I hadn't checked on him, the accident would've never been reported. I also had a school bus pull out in front of me on a residential road in Maryland. The road was a little icy and I was coming around a bend. I pulled the lever for the trailer brakes so I wouldn't jackknife. The trailer skidded off the road and through someone's front yard, while the tractor stayed in the lane. I came to a stop about 10 feet from hitting the bus. I guess the bus driver panicked, and stopped halfway onto the road. It finally got out of my way, and I dragged my trailer back onto the road. Another time, I was speeding a little on 95 in Maryland and a state cop pulled out after me. He was gaining fast as I exited at the Glen Burnie exit. There was a big piece of firewood in the middle of the lane, and I let it go between my wheels. The cop had just turned on the flashing lights when the firewood wedged up under his car. I saw the front of his car lift up, and he had to pull off. What a lucky break!

We did a big moving job in DC, and I got injured again. We were maneuvering a tall piece of furniture through a narrow doorway, and we knocked the glass exit sign off the ceiling. It shattered on my head, and it was about a half inch thick glass. I believe this was the third or fourth concussion that I've had. When my head stopped spinning, the boss was trying to help me up. I told him I needed to get the glass out of my eye first. I went into the men's room and used a piece of toilet paper to pick the glass shard off my eyeball. And I had to get a piece out of my eye. My forehead was sliced open above my eye. The boss told his son to take me to the hospital. Georgetown University Hospital removed a lot of glass from my head and did a lot of stitching. They told me they had to leave some of the glass in there, but it wouldn't hurt me.

We moved a group of gay men into a townhouse in DC, and after the move, they invited us to get high with them. I turned down the offer and waited outside, while the other guys smoked weed and drank beer. As I was waiting outside, the lady told me she was with the welcome wagon. She asked if the lady of the house was around, and I explained that he was busy right now. I don't know if she got the meaning of that.

We also did several divorce moves. The man and woman would be fighting over who got what. We just sat out on the truck since we got paid by the hour.

Occasionally, the boss would have me train a new driver. I hated this because most of them were high school kids. One kid almost flipped over the loaded moving van on an exit ramp. Another kid left the truck in neutral with the parking brake off, at the loading dock of BWI airport. We were unloading the truck, and all of a sudden, the truck wasn't there. It was rolling across the tarmac of the airport. I ran right off the loading dock and chased the truck down. I stopped it right before it went over an embankment. I told the boss I was done being a truck driver Instructor.

We moved a load of antique furniture to New Orleans. I dropped the trailer off and we went to the French Quarter. It was me and Chris, the boss's son. We were walking down Bourbon Street and Chris says "wow look at the hot girl in the doorway". He went in and came back out quickly. I told him "Hey next time read the sign.". The sign above the bar said, "female impersonators". We were switching off on driving the truck back, and every time I dozed off in the passenger seat, he threw a fire cracker at my feet.

After dropping off a load of airmail at BWI, I was on my way back, and just as I was crossing the Cabin John bridge, I saw a lady in a black dress. She was leaning over the railing of the bridge, and the next thing I saw was her going over the railing. I couldn't believe what I had just seen, and I stopped my truck and got out. When I looked over the railing, she was just hitting the water of the Potomac river. She was still alive and trying to swim. I told a trucker to radio for help. Everybody had a CB radio back then. There were other people trying to help her too. One guy went down the bank on the Virginia side and another guy went down the Maryland side. Somehow, she swam to the Maryland side and I guess she was OK. Now the bridge is called the American Legion Memorial Bridge. I had traffic blocked for about a half an hour, but if I hadn't stopped, I don't think anyone would've seen her jump, since it happened right next to my truck in slow-moving traffic.

Another day, a guy in a small truck swerved off the road and drove through a crowded yard sale. I stopped to help there, too, but there was nothing I could do. Everybody somehow had gotten out of the way. A father snatched his child up out of the crib but could not save the other child in the crib. I was sickened and traumatized by such a senseless tragedy. It's something I wish I had never witnessed. I was still shaking when I picked up the mail at Dulles airport.

I used to enjoy watching the Concorde take off from Dulles. It was a supersonic plane, and it only used about a third of the airstrip to take off. It flew at 1300 mph and it got to London in two hours.

I was living two lives. One as a hard-working truck driver, and mover. I would also be the mechanic for a growing fleet of trucks and trailers. But on the weekends, I lived the life of an addict and an alcoholic. Monday mornings were hell!. I hated the sound of birds chirping, because it meant it was time to go to work. Coming down from cocaine is a terrible depressed feeling along with inability to sleep. A hard day's work would burn that off and I'd be ready for beers on Monday night. My routine on weekdays was to come home and smoke some pot, drink some beer, and play my guitar. I loved playing Southern rock, like Lynyrd Skynyrd, the Outlaws, Molly Hatchet, etc. I had a friend named Jeff, who usually jammed with me. He played a left-handed Guild guitar. His friend, Wayne, joined our band as a singer. We would record our jam sessions on cassette tapes. They were both movers too, and did the same things I did.

I was experiencing some blackouts from drinking too much, and I was depressed and even suicidal at times. I was worried about having guns around, so I took them all to a gun store. One was a Winchester, model 97, that my grandfather had given me. I hated to see it go, but my plan was to buy a nice guitar with the money. I bought a 75 Stratocaster from my friend, Joe. I had a Fender deluxe reverb amp, and it sounded pretty good. Wayne, Jeff and I would jam on weekends. Wayne started wrecking his car often from drinking. One night he scraped the bottom of his car and ripped off the shifter linkage. I rigged the shifter into drive so the car would only go forward. I told him to buy a new shift cable, but he never did. I also warned him that he was going to kill somebody, the way he drove drunk. We were at a house I was renting in the country, and I took up a collection to go get some coke. Wayne was playing "That Smell" by Skynyrd, and I had never heard him play that good. It was the last song he would ever play. When I got back with the drugs and alcohol, Wayne was dead.

There were state troopers and an ambulance in the front yard. His car was up on a railroad tie that bordered the property. He had wrecked into the railroad tie and crawled under his car to put it in reverse. Unfortunately, he had backed the car over his neck and suffocated. It's a very odd feeling when you are high as a kite, but your friend has just died. I blamed myself for making his car drivable in the first place. In the future, I turned down repair jobs for people who drank heavy or smoked PCP. There was a funeral and a family get together for Wayne and everybody was drinking. I felt the opposite, and I didn't drink, because that's what killed him. Jeff and I would jam sometimes, but it wasn't the same without Wayne. At the funeral, a bird landed on my hood, and it just stared at me for a while. Then it flew off, and I thought it was a sign. We played "Free Bird" many times.

I did a lot of side jobs on my friend's cars and I got a reputation as a good mechanic. I was recommended to a guy in Alexandria who had a 68 Corvette. It had a 427 with 435 hp, but it had sat for years, and the engine was locked up. I really enjoyed working on nice cars like this one. It was white with a four-speed transmission. I pulled the engine and brought it to Fairfax to rebuild it. I pulled one piston at a time to unfreeze it. Then I had it bored out and machined. I completely rebuilt it with a few upgrades for more horsepower. I put the engine back in and took his wife for a ride. He was still at work. The car was so fast it even scared me a little. I only gave it about three-quarter throttle. It had chrome side pipes, and it sounded great! I made a mental note not to race against it. They were thrilled with the finished product and paid me well.

I had brief times like this where I stayed clean and relatively sober. My philosophy was that I wasn't selling drugs like some of my friends were. I was working like some of my friends weren't. I wasn't hurting anyone but myself, and that was my choice to make.

My dog, Natasha, or Tasha, as I called her, was my only true friend. She was teething, and I let her rip up my cardboard 12 pack cartons. I could go to a party and tell her "get the beer", and she would steal someone's 12 pack, and bring it to me by the handle. I taught her how to do this and people thought it was hilarious.

I had a box to deliver to Winchester, Virginia, one day, and I took the bosses Datsun 510 instead of the truck. On the way back I was rolling down Route 50 at about 60 mph. An old guy pulled out right in front of me from a side road. I knew I could never stop in time, and I would have hit him right in the driver side door. All I could do was crank the steering wheel to my left and I hope I missed him. I must've missed him by an inch or two, and the Datsun was on two wheels, going into a wide grass median with a low point in the middle of it. I hit the lowest point of the median and the car bounced onto the left two wheels. I was headed towards the oncoming traffic, and I was up on the left two wheels. Somehow, I came back down onto all four wheels and steered right to avoid a head on collision. My adrenaline was pumping, and I was pissed! I turned around and chased the old man down. I basically ran him off onto the shoulder of the road. He was driving a Belvedere wagon with Quebec tags on it. I popped his hood and pulled out all his spark plug wires. His glasses were like Coke bottles and his wife was screaming at me.

I pulled all the plug wires for two reasons. One, I didn't want him endangering anyone else, and two, I would have to find a payphone to call the police. The boss's car was damaged, and I wanted him to be accountable for the damage. When the cop finally got there, the guy from Quebec was gone. Somebody had probably put the plug wires back on. I had his tag number, and I gave it to the cop. He made an accident report, and I showed him where it happened. The scene of the accident showed exactly what happened. There were two skid marks, turning left where I had to crank the wheel. In the grass median strip, there was one track where I was on the two right wheels. Then at the bottom of the median, there were two tracks where the car bounced up on the left two wheels. There was one track again going up toward the oncoming traffic. Altogether, the car had gone about 50 yards on two wheels. The cop asked me if I was some kind of thrill seeker, and he couldn't believe I rode that one out. I couldn't believe it either. Anyone else would've probably slammed that guy and his driver door and we'd all be dead. I was lucky to survive that one!

I continued to drive the air mail route from Dulles to BWI airport. The beltway around DC was a nightmare. People just wanted to come out of my blind spot, and pass me. Then they would hit their brakes in front of me. I guess they thought I could stop on a dime. I did some real driving a few times to avoid idiots. I remember one car that cut in front of me and slammed on their brakes. There was an African American young boy in the backseat. I slammed on my brakes and came within inches of rear ending them. I can still see that boy's face, so close in front of me. His eyes were as big as baseballs, and I swear his skin turned white! On the way home, I would stop at Chantilly cash and carry, and get a 12 pack to calm my nerves. That was a cool little store that seemed to have everything. My drinking and drugging were getting worse and the boss was getting irritated with me. I did a pretty good job of covering it up, but his two sons would see me at parties and I'm pretty sure Chris probably told him. One day he told me he was letting me go.

After 10 years or more, I had just gotten written off. My share of his profit- sharing plan was a measly 275 bucks. I'm pretty sure I got screwed on that too. I have broken my back for these people, and risked my life on the highway. A few months earlier, I had been hack-sawing the stack on the tractor trailer and gotten a metal splinter in my cornea. I called in sick to have eye surgery the next morning. The boss's wife thought I was making it up, until I handed her the doctor bill. I went back to work with a patch on my eye. Anyway, goodbye A+A Transfer co. I really couldn't blame them, but some of my other friends had gotten into rehab, or some type of treatment with the help of their boss or their company. As the structure in my life fell away, things got worse and worse. I was hanging out with some friends, and somebody had some Thorazine pills. I've never heard of them, and they said to take two or three. I took four and went out driving around. I got drowsy, and pulled into a townhouse complex. I parked my car and fell asleep. I woke up three days later with one hell of a backache. My battery was dead, so I borrowed one from a nearby car. I thought it was the next day, but then I found out that three days had passed. I also found out that Thorazine was for severe mental patients. I had taken a nearly fatal dose. I had a bad habit of experimenting with pot, cocaine, heroin, mescaline, Quaaludes, Nebutol, Percocet, Darvocet, alcohol, LSD, Thorazine, and God knows what else I did. I would mix different drugs, and there was always alcohol in the mix. It's a wonder I survived.

Meanwhile, Christine was coming back around. I guess the dead-head guy dumped her. I had picked up an 18-foot camper and parked it on my parent's property. I had just dropped out of college at Lord Fairfax community college. I guess I'll backtrack a little to that fiasco. Since my right arm was disabled from reconstructive surgery, my dad talked me into college. I wanted to get into automotive electronics, so I took two electronics classes plus the regular classes. I lived in the camper at Cedar creek campground with my dog, Tasha. I was writing all my assignments left-handed. I rode a 10-speed bicycle down the mountain to school in Middletown. I almost got a speeding ticket coming down the mountain on the bicycle when I went through a radar trap. I forgot what he clocked me at, but he let it slide. I dropped my English class because they wanted me to give a speech. My social anxiety was too bad for that. After that, it all went downhill, and I quit. I always hated school.

CHAPTER 10

BEING STALKED
BY CHRISTINE

Anyway, I was back in Fairfax, and Christine was coming around. I made the mistake of thinking we could work things out. I was riding with her one day, and we got into an argument. I got out of the car at the bottom of my parent's street, and started walking. She threw my guitar out her window onto the street. Then she dumped out a bag of my dog food! Then she came at me, swinging at me. I raised my arms to block her punches, and she finally quit. I retreated to my camper and my dog for some peace and quiet.

The next day, she was waiting down the street, stalking me. I saw her and came back home. Later, I heard all kinds of commotion outside. Christine had stood in front of her Opel Kadett, and let it run her over! My dad and some of the neighbors were lifting the car off of her. She was hospitalized for burns from the exhaust pipe. I visited her in the hospital and I guess I felt sorry for her. I was stupid! We ended up back together and living in a trailer park on route 1 in Alexandria, Virginia.

The last straw with Christine was when my friend Eric told me what Christine told him. She told him she had gone to DC and shot up Dilaudid with some guy. When I confronted her about it, she lied, as usual, and I lifted her shirt sleeve. There was a big X scraped into her arm, and she had missed covering up the needle mark. She told me she had an accident with scissors. I told her to quit lying, and that Eric told me all about it. She stuck to her lie. With the aids virus in full swing and people dying, I knew this was the end of me and Christine. If she was sharing needles, I was done.

On the way home from her house, I was telling her we were done. She came to a red light at Woodson high school, and began to turn right on red. My house was to the left, and I knew she would take me as far from my house as she could. I jumped out of the car and she stopped. I was going to walk home, but I realized my dog was still in the car. I went to open the passenger door, but she locked it from the inside. Then I reached through the window, which was down about 6 inches. She rolled my arm up in the window and started driving off. This was my right arm which just had reconstructive surgery for nerve, artery, and tendon damage. My adrenaline rushed as she dragged me down route 236 and my feet were about to go under the back wheel. With my left arm, I bent the door outwards until the glass broke, and I fell onto the road. She stopped the car, and I grabbed Tasha, my dog. I started running towards the high school, but she caught up and jumped on my back. She bit two chunks of skin out of my back, but I finally got free. I made it to the high school, and hid in some bushes to rest. She was in her car flagging people down. She stopped two guys and sent them after me. I'm sure she told them some wild story for attention and pity.

They found me resting because Tasha barked. They were a little scared to fight because of Tasha growling. I showed them the bite marks, and my right arm was in bad shape. I'm glad they realized that I was the victim. As I walked home the back way, I could see the police arriving on the scene. I ended up facing an assault charge, which dragged on for about six months. I withdrew from everybody and had ulcers from worrying. I hired a lawyer, who learned that Christine was having severe mental health issues, which I had never known the extent of. When I appeared in court, they tried to confuse me, by referring to my right arm, but I corrected them. "No, I broke the door off her car with my left arm." The car was cheaply made, but I was amazed at the damage to the right door. I had bent the top of the door frame, 8 inches outward. The judge asked me about Christine's bruises on her arms, and I explained that she had just beaten me at the bottom of my parents street, in an earlier incident. I had statements from the neighbors on three corners of the intersection, who witnessed that. One neighbor was subpoenaed. She testified that Christine threw my guitar in the street, dumped out my dog food, struck me repeatedly. She also testified that I raised my arms, only to protect myself, and did not strike her.

I told the judge that the bruises on her arms were from her striking me. I had pictures of the bite marks. When my lawyer asked Christine about her psychiatrist, she flew off the handle, and, everyone saw her true colors. My social anxiety, plus 6 months of worrying, made me very nervous in court. The judge probably took that as a sign of guilt. At the end of the hearing, he said "I don't believe either one of you, but I'm dismissing this case." At least it was over. I felt insulted that he didn't believe me, but at least it was over. After a brief period of being single, I caved in again to her, wanting me back. It sounds like the battered wife syndrome, where the woman keeps forgiving her abuser. I guess I had the battered boyfriend syndrome. Or I was just plain stupid. I kept thinking she could change, but she didn't.

We were back to living in my 18-foot camper at the trailer park. We had a neighbor who was selling a 40-foot trailer in the same park.

I had mine sold for $1200, and Christine really liked the bigger home. We packed up our stuff and my plan was working well. Christine was as violent as ever, and I knew I had to escape her. I put together another Camaro, and she still had the Opel Kadett. I got $1200 cash for my trailer, and had the money in my pocket. As she packed boxes, I put her stuff in her car, and my stuff in my car. When we were all loaded up, I burned rubber out of there. I headed for California, where my sister Tami lived in San Diego.

I felt like the weight of the world was off of me, as I hit the highway in my 70 Camaro, and $1200 in my pocket. Gas was $1.20 a gallon, and I even had a bag of weed with me. I stopped at a rest area and smoked a joint. I started to feel bad for Christine, and what I had done. I must've been stoned! I guess after being with her for a few years, I got attached, despite her craziness. I quickly dismissed my change of heart and got back on the highway. It was a nice cruise going cross country. My parents had retired to Kansas, but I headed straight to California. On my way. I heard the news that Ronald Reagan had been shot. This was March 30, 1981.

It was beautiful scenery on route 40 west. I went through Arkansas, Oklahoma City, Amarillo, Texas, Albuquerque, Winslow, Arizona, the Indian reservations, and then route eight into San Diego. Tami didn't know I was coming, and she was quite surprised when she opened her door! I probably should've told her I was coming, but her and I had a habit of practical jokes and surprises. She had a roommate who had a boyfriend, and I was kind of in the way, so I did a lot of walking around exploring. I was used to the southern hospitality of Virginia, and this place just seemed very cold. I would see house parties everywhere, but they would tell me I wasn't invited. I had to keep Tasha on a leash, and I rented a pair of roller skates and let her pull me around. I hit the boardwalk and set a speed record for roller skating. Tasha was a shepherd, husky, and part coyote. I must've been doing about 30 miles an hour when she saw another dog. She swerved to the right of someone and I would have to drop the leash, and go to the left that person, and then pick up the leash and keep going. We had a lot of fun on the boardwalk.

I walked across the street between two intersections, and a cop on a bicycle wrote me a ticket for jaywalking. I told him I had only been here a couple days, but he wrote me up anyway. He told me I had to appear in court the following week. When I went to court, people were charged with serious offenses, and people laughed when they read my charge. I think it was only 20 bucks or something. I found a tiny garage to park my Camaro in, and fix a few things on it. Mostly, I wandered the beach, checking out the ladies. I was out of pot, and I asked a couple of people where I could get some. Mostly what people had was called "tie" or "Thai" or something. It was like $20 for a little bud. Tami took Tasha for a walk on the beach, and somehow, Tasha got lost. I was heartbroken! I had raised her from a puppy. While I was driving around looking for her, I met a guy who was selling a quarter pound of pot. I bought it for around 200 bucks, and the next thing I knew, I was surrounded by cops. I was set up like a bowling pin, as the Grateful Dead song goes. They threw me in a cop car and I watched as another cop burned rubber with my car.

They threw me in the LA Jolla jail, and my car went to the impound. It seems like everyone spoke Spanish, except me, in there. Tami picked me up the next morning, and I retrieved my car. She was a bartender at a really nice bar and she knew a lawyer. He said that my best bet was to leave San Diego. Since I was visiting anyway, and it was only a misdemeanor. I was searching dog pounds for Tasha, and I finally found her! She was so happy to see me, she was squealing and barking. The vet knew that she was my dog immediately. She had been hit by a car and was picked up right by my sister's house. I was amazed she had found her way to Tami's house, because it was row after row of identical houses, all the way down at the beach. She was all banged up and couldn't walk. I paid the vet $450 and carried her to my car. I felt like I couldn't leave there fast enough! I said goodbye to Tami, and apologized for being such a pain.

I was so glad to see the "entering Arizona" sign. It was also the beginning of me feeling that they would catch up to me. From this time forward, I lived under the radar. My money was about gone, and I knew I would have to sell the Camaro to get home, wherever home was. I stopped in Yuma, Arizona, and got a hotel room. I sold the Camaro, and bought a junky Impala. I was nursing Tasha back to health in the hotel room, while a biker rally came into town.

The Impala made it to Albuquerque, New Mexico, and then the engine blew. I was in a predicament, to say the least. The bus and the train wouldn't take Tasha. I had a couple hundred bucks left, and I rented a car at a place called "rent a heap, cheap". It was a big old Buick with cruise control. I loaded Tasha and my stuff, and hit the road. My plan was to make it to Kansas, where my parents were. When I called my dad, he said Christine was calling to find out where I was. My stepmother, Ida, was slipping further into schizophrenia. He had to have her committed to a hospital in Leavenworth. The "heap" was running hot when I went through the hills and mountains. Luckily, there were barrels of water along the highway. I made it to Kansas and dropped off Tasha. Then the plan was to return the rental car, and ride the bus back to Kansas. I stopped at a gas station in Oklahoma, and I met some cool people. They invited me to a party, where I found some LSD. It was a cool party, and a big change from the cold people of San Diego. It was hard to leave, but I hit the highway with a major buzz going, and the cruise control on.

The Buick was overheating bad at this point, and I tried every trick I knew to get it back to New Mexico. I barely made it, and I pulled into a car wash by the car rental. I washed the car and let the engine cool down completely. I filled the radiator with cold water and returned the car. They looked it over and gave me my deposit back. I asked him if he could give me a ride to the bus station, and he said OK. To my dismay, he hopped in the Buick, and I hopped into the passenger side. When he dropped me off, I barely made my bus. As the bus drove away, I looked out the window. The Buick was blowing steam from under the hood. The guy was opening the hood, and then a huge cloud of steam erupted. I couldn't help but laugh. What a heap!

CHAPTER 11

BACK TO KANSAS

It was a long bus ride to Kansas. I just wanted to stretch out my back, but the seats only recline about 2 inches. I ended up staying in my parent's Winnebago with them. That was a real drag, but eventually, I moved into the small garage where I fixed equipment. My dad had contractors building his house on a lot at Lake Perry country club. There was a golf course, and I got a job fixing all the mowers, golf carts, tractors, trucks, etc. I went through an episode of bleeding ulcers, and that was rough.

Eventually, I could eat toast and started getting better. I met some friends who worked on the golf course, and one of them was growing pot on the fringes of the golf course. They called it K weed, I guess the K stood for Kansas. I saved up enough money to build another Camaro. I got the shell at an auction for $40. Then I got a motor and transmission for $75. I did a brief stint in a rock band and played the local skating rink. On one of our gigs, I had just wrecked on a dirt bike that I had fixed. My knee was skinned bad when I did a wheelie off a jump, and the bike came out from under me. I did a "superman," flying through the air and came down hard on my front side. I had to go to the hospital, and they bandaged my knee. I got a quart of beer and barely made it to the gig on time. I had to change my jeans because they were all ripped up and bloody. As I was playing my guitar, people were looking pointing at my leg. I looked down, and there was a big blood spot that was getting bigger and bigger. My knee was still bleeding badly. At night I would ride into Topeka and party with the workers at the Hallmark card factory who got off at 2 AM. One night, I was coming home wasted in my dad's Granada and plowed through a cornfield. That woke me up, and I got it home with no damage. My Camaro was about done, and I couldn't wait to leave Kansas. I was still mad at my dad for selling my first Camaro while I was away at college. It was wrecked in the front, but it was fixable. I had it parked in his backyard under the tree I had used to change six different engines into it. I paid $2750 for it and he sold it for $50. Anyway, as soon as I fired this one up, I put a note in my dad's mailbox, and hit the highway.

CHAPTER 12

BACK TO VIRGINIA

I rode into Virginia the same way I had rolled out, about six months earlier, driving a Camaro. It was the same color, and people thought it was the same car. I hung out with some of my friends in the Six Shooter Band. Joe was practicing at Ross's house, and they liked the "K weed" that I had brought back from Kansas. My friends looked at me differently because Christine had spread lies about me being abusive. She was a chronic liar, and always had some kind of sob story to make people feel sorry for her. She claimed her brother and her father and her ex-boyfriend also abused her, which wasn't true. Of all of the bad things she had done, this really ticked me off. I tried for years to help her, and she dragged my name through the mud. Despite my drug use, I had very high moral values, and I respected women (except maybe my stepmother).

CHAPTER 13

OLIVER'S STRIKE 2

There was a bar called Oliver's in downtown Fairfax, that hosted some big names in music. My friends in the Six Shooter Band would play there a lot, and they would pack the house. A couple times I was the doorman, and I would collect the cover charge. A lot of famous musicians played there, and I partied with a few of them. I also went to a great show at a nearby bar in Springfield, Virginia. It was a small place, and I saw The Outlaws, Foghat, Leslie West of Mountain, Blue Cheer, and Toy Caldwell of the Marshall Tucker band. The amazing thing was that there were only about 25 people in the audience. I remember standing mesmerized in front of Hughie Thomasson of The Outlaws, while he played the hell out of his Stratocaster. It was a great show!

One night at Oliver's, a few of us went out to my friend Debbie's car to catch a buzz. A few bikers walked up and flashed a badge in my face. I was snorting some coke and they busted us. I had 1/10 of a gram, $10 worth. Then I was at the police station, they wanted me to rat on the person I got it from, I refused. They kept bugging me with scare tactics, etc. because it had tested at a very high purity level. It was straight from a Miami drug cartel. I went to court and the judge asked me if a coke spoon was mine. I said yes, even though it wasn't. Then he asked me why Debbie had a whole coke kit in her purse, minus the spoon. I took full responsibility for my choices, and then some. My philosophy was that if I never sold drugs, and if I wanted to take them myself, then that was my right. He sentenced me to 30 days. It was actually 12 months with 11 suspended. This was strike two, at a time when three strikes was a long prison term.

CHAPTER 14

MORE HEARTBREAK

As if all this wasn't enough to drive me nuts, there was more bad news. I was living in an old, abandoned boat at a friend's house. I went out for one reason or another, and when I came back, Tasha had been hit by a car. Another friend of mine was there, and he was very upset. I had a feeling that he was the one who hit her. The house was a drug hotspot and there was a lot of traffic. I had put Tasha on her leash, but someone must have let her off. I was devastated! Tasha was gone. She was my only family at the time. I had nursed her back to health after the San Diego incident and had her for about five years. I even went clear to Culpeper, Virginia, to steal her back from Christine, who had stolen her from me. I remember when she had her pups in my bedroom and tore my couch to shreds. I looked under my bed, because I heard a noise, and she growled at me for the first time. She was protecting her pups. The father of the pups had jumped in my car window, and when I came out of 7-Eleven with my morning coffee, they were humping in the front seat. I pulled into work, and all the guys were laughing. So many good times. R.I.P. Tasha.

CHAPTER 15

30 DAYS IN THE HOLE

Being in jail is rough for a free-spirited person. Luckily, I got into a work release program. There was a guy named Ron, who hired inmates for his moving company. I fixed up a couple of old trucks and went on some moving jobs. I was working on the opposite side of the parking lot from A+A. Every day I had to piss in a cup when I got back. It was hard for me to do, with someone watching. I had to drink massive amounts of fluids to pull it off. I felt much better in this brief period of sobriety, but the rest of it sucked. A couple of my cellmates and I got an apartment and the party was back on for me. My friend Steve took me to DC to celebrate my release. We walked into a building and the next thing I knew I was standing in the center of a circle of half-naked women. He told me to take my pick, he was buying. I picked a beautiful girl and had a brief session of safe sex. I came out and waited around for Steve. I guess he was getting busy too. It was so easy to get a hooker, but I couldn't get a girlfriend to save my life. I would have so much rather had a girlfriend who wasn't psycho. I'm definitely not proud of my affairs with prostitutes. I believe I needed some form of love, even if it wasn't real.

CHAPTER 16

BACK TO THE PARTY

Pretty soon, I was back to my old habits. Nights of partying, and agonizing mornings. After doing coke all night, I would try to sleep, but I couldn't. I used to hate the sound of the birds chirping in the morning. It was time to drag my dead ass out of bed and move a four-bedroom house. There's no worse feeling in the world! The coke would make me grind my teeth and clench my jaw. I could barely talk. I truly believe that my cocaine addiction started at about the age of 12 when the plastic surgeons broke my nose with a metal fork and a hammer and then packed it full of gauze strips, treated with pharmaceutical cocaine. When I would get to work half dead, I couldn't talk. The guys would look at me like, "what the hell is wrong with you?" After about four hours of hard work, I would start to feel better. Ron was a good guy to work for, and most of the time, I had my act together. There were some fun times, and a lot of good mover stories. My friend Scotty always made us laugh. Once he pulled Al's shorts down while he was carrying one end of a couch. The homeowner's daughter was standing there laughing. Al couldn't go anywhere with his shorts around his ankles. Luckily, he was wearing underwear. I saw Scotty at a Halloween party and he had the backside of his pants cut out. He was walking around mooning everybody. He was one funny dude.

CHAPTER 17

THE PURPLE SPIKE HEADS

I was still living in the apartment, and I had an opportunity to be the middleman in a coke deal. I didn't consider this selling; I was just picking up a quarter ounce, and passing it on to someone else. My plan was to take a small cut for myself. Once I started taking snorts of coke from the bag, I couldn't stop. I kept telling myself just one more. But like they say, monkeys can't sell bananas. I hopped on a bus to Georgetown, which is a section of DC with lots of bars, along M St. I was looking for an out-of-the-way place to snort some more coke. I went under the bridge there, and there was a whole party going on! It was a bunch of kids with spiked hairdos. There were purple ones, pink ones and you name it, they were wild. I hung out with them, secretly dipping into the bag every five minutes. Eventually, I rode the bus back to Fairfax, as paranoia set in.

There is a condition known as cocaine induced psychosis. It's common among chronic users, and it's similar to schizophrenia. Anyway, I got off the bus and hid in the woods, doing more coke. I thought the cops were after me, and I got back on a different bus to throw them off my trail. Eventually, I was back at Fairfax Circle, where the trucks were parked. I hid inside one of Ron's trucks, the old blue one. I swear I heard people on top of the truck, cutting their way into the truck. I hid under some moving pads, but the nightmare continued. I remember yelling at a guy who was putting gas in his car at the Memco gas station on the other side of the fence. He looked at me like I was crazy. I was, I had snorted $700 worth of Coke in about a day, and there would be hell to pay. I finally got my head back together and evaluated the mess I was in. I needed to pay some people back, which, eventually, I did. I never seemed to learn my lesson. I would go about a week and then crave the feeling that coke gave me. I would always tell myself it'll be different this time. It was different. It was worse each time.

CHAPTER 18

STICK UP

I was hanging out at the 7-Eleven on University Drive, in Fairfax, one night. Luckily, they didn't remember me as the guy who stole some tasty cakes years earlier. At the time, I was extremely hungry, and we weren't fed at home. They chased me down the street, but never caught me. Anyway, I was hanging out, and I had a small amount of coke on me. I was trying to get a ride to a party or something, and a girl pulled in with a rough looking dude in the passenger seat. It's funny how one addict can spot another. He told me to jump on in when I said, "Where is the party?". I jumped in the backseat, and he asked me where he could get some coke. I told him I had a little bit, but I could get more. I had about a quarter of a gram, and I pulled it out and did a snort with a little cut off straw. The next thing I know he turns around in the front passenger seat and points a huge pistol at my head! In the words of Ronnie van Zandt, "it ain't no fun, staring straight down a 44". I proceeded to snort the whole bag in one snort. Then I gave him the empty bag. Part of that was courage, and part of that was not caring about myself anymore. The rest of that was the power of addiction.

We were in the grocery store parking lot, across the street from 711. He yelled at me to get out, and I gladly did just that. His girl-friend drove in circles around me, while he hung out the window, pointing the gun at me. I was thinking he would shoot, but he never did. Eventually they left.

I was at a time in my life where I became suicidal. I felt like I had been put on this earth to be tortured. I must have done something really bad in the past life or something. I didn't see drugs and alcohol as the cause of these problems. I saw it as the solution to the problems. I had sold a couple rifles to the gun store because I didn't trust myself with them. I would have blackouts and not remember the night before. One of the rifles was a Winchester model 97 that my grandfather had given me. I hated to sell them, but I knew I should. I bought my first Fender Stratocaster with the money. I still had a small pistol from my grandfather, and I came close to shooting myself one night. I called my friend Lynn and she cheered me up. She was my only true friend at that time. I gave the pistol to a friend who collected guns.

CHAPTER 19

SMOOTHER MOVERS

Around that time, I got a job with Smoother Movers. Some people used to say the name sounded more like a laxative, than a moving company. Steve was the boss, and he was cool. We had a crew of good old boys, and a girl named Tammy, who worked as hard as the guys did. I remember the song by Dire Straits came out "money for nothing" at that time. We would be riding in the truck singing along. "We got to move these refrigerators, we got to move these color TVs." Whenever someone dropped a TV or something, we would say "smooth move, Ex-Lax". I moved to Leesburg, Virginia, to be closer to work which was in Sterling. I moved into a three-story apartment complex with my friend Kenny and his wife. She had just had a baby. I picked up a 72 Ford truck with toolboxes on the back, and I made a lot of side money doing auto and truck repairs. My party lifestyle seemed to use up my money as fast as I made it. There was an Irish pub in the shopping center called "Shenanigans". One night I met a girl that I will call Phyllis. I won't use her real name. She was rather large, and not very attractive, but alcohol has a way of changing that.

The first night I met her, she showed me a lake where everybody skinny-dipped. It was like a nudist colony. There were lots of pretty girls. I tried to find this place again, but I never found it.

CHAPTER 20

TAKING PHYLLIS HOME

I ran into Phyllis again at the bar one night, and we drank a bunch of Jack and cokes. At closing time, the plan was for her to come home with me. We were both plastered. My apartment complex was behind the bar, so we walked in the back way. My section of the building was the last one to the right side. It was the only section that was recessed back a little from the rest. When coming in the back way, I thought I was at the last section. I wasn't. I was at the second to last section. We went up the stairs to the third floor, but my key wouldn't open the door. I told her to wait there, and I would climb the balconies and let her in. I climbed up the balconies like Spider-Man, and went in through the sliding door. I stumbled through the living room in the dark and let her in. We went down the hallway to my room, where I opened the door and turned on the light. The room was pink, and a girl woke up, screaming. All the sudden it hit me! I was in the wrong apartment! I could hear adults coming from the master bedroom. My first instinct was to get the hell out of there! The hallway wasn't wide enough for me and Phyllis. As I reversed my direction towards the door, Phyllis fell backwards into the coffee table. I heard the sound of breaking wood as I went out the door. I saw her stuck there, with her butt wedged in the coffee table. I flew down the steps and figured out where I lived real quick. Poor Phyllis, she never should have drank with a fool like me. Whenever I would come and go into my apartment, I would hide my face, and I never heard any more about it. At least until the next time I saw Phyllis at the bar. She was not happy.

CHAPTER 21

WRONG HOUSE

I had a few times when I woke up in the wrong house, and didn't know how I got there. One time, I woke up, sleeping on the couch, and I looked around at my surroundings. There were pictures on the wall of Asian people. I was very dehydrated, and I opened the refrigerator to see Asian beer and food. I grabbed a beer, and snuck quietly out the door. I figured either I had walked into the wrong apartment, or some good Samaritan had let me sleep on the couch. I wasn't going to stick around and find out.

Another time I was drinking with my friend, Randy, in Burke, Virginia. He lived in a row of town houses, and I woke up two doors down on someone's couch. When I woke up, they were asking me who I was, and why I was in their house. I remember saying, "where am I?" and feeling like a complete idiot. I walked out of there feeling about 2 feet tall. I was lucky that I wasn't shot.

CHAPTER 22

MOTHER MARY

I was still in Leesburg, working for Smoother Movers, and still doing drugs and alcohol on every payday. I became very sick, with what, I don't know. Thank God for a woman named Mary who worked at 7-Eleven. She was a friend of my coworkers, and she took me in. There was an extra room in her house, where I laid in bed for about a week. She would bring me soup and nursed me back to health. I have never been that sick before. I sweated pools of sweat, and she would wash the sheets almost every day. I believe I came very close to dying, and this Angel of Mercy had saved my life. I often wonder why she was there at just the right time, and I truly believe she was part of God's plan, a guardian angel, if you will. I only saw her a couple of times after that, when I was in that neighborhood, and stopped by the 7-Eleven. I would thank her for saving my life, but she would just shrug it off. Thank you again, Mary! You're an angel!

CHAPTER 23

ANOTHER DUI

I was still driving the 72 Ford truck, and I was coming back from a party at Harper's Ferry. My headlights were blinking on and off. A passing cop turned around and pulled me over. I had just finished the last beer in a six pack. He gave me the whole sobriety test. I had to stand up, tilt my head back, and extend my arms. Then he gave me the breathalyzer test. It came to .10, which was borderline drunk in their opinion. After a night in the Loudon county jail, they gave me a court date, and sent me on my way. We called it low down county, With Leesburg (Sleazeburg) in the middle. Eventually, the court date came around. I went in front of the judge, and he asked a few questions. He asked me about my previous DUI and I told him about the ASAP program, and how they taught me how to calculate my blood alcohol content (BAC). According to my body weight and the number of beers I had, I could drink two beers per hour, and stay under the legal limit of .10. I even showed him the papers from the ASAP class. He said "well, we certainly have learned a lot about the ASAP program" and shook his head. He asked me about the sobriety test and asked me to demonstrate it. I told him I had a severe injury to my left foot, which made it a little harder to walk a straight line. When I stood up and tilted my head back, and extended my arms, I heard a loud gasp from the court room. They saw the scar across my right wrist where I had the injury, and the reconstructive surgery. The judge asked me if the officer had a flashlight. I said no. He dismissed the case, and I was so happy that I went and got drunk!

CHAPTER 24

MORE BELTWAY BLUES

I met a guy in the area named Tony. He had an 18-wheeler with a dump trailer, and he offered me a job. He gave me an on-the-spot driving test, to see if I could drive it. I had no problem driving it, I just needed to get used to the 13 speed transmission. Shifting the gears was a learning experience, but I caught on quickly. I started immediately, hauling sand and gravel. I would pick up a load of sand going into La Plata, Maryland. Then I would drive about 5 miles to pick up the gravel, which came back to Occoquan, VA. It was a whole different ball game when you're hauling 26 tons on each trip. I needed a lot more stopping distance, and I fried the brake shoes quite often. I was replacing brakes regularly. I had six loads a day, which was three round trips. I was on the other half of the beltway from what I was used to. I used to cross the Cabin John bridge, which is now the American Legion Bridge. Now I was crossing the Woodrow Wilson bridge. I would have to fly down the Virginia side to make the uphill climb on the Maryland side. The bridge seemed rickety, and the pavement was uneven. I had to fight the steering wheel to get across the bridge. It was highly stressful! I got paid by the ton and I was hauling about 150 tons a day.

It was a little scary when I would dump the sand and gravel. A lot of guys would tip their trucks over if one side of the load slid out before the other side. I would be next to the truck, working the levers and ready to jump out of the way. It was critical to have the truck on level ground. I did this for about six months before it all came to an end.

CHAPTER 25

JACKKNIFE

I was heading down route seven out of Leesburg one morning, on my way to pick up the first load. My roommate, Kenny, wanted to ride along. I was coming down a hill, towards a major intersection, and my light turned from green to yellow. I started to hit the brakes lightly, and my left front brake locked up. This sent the whole truck a little to the left and I had to let off the brake to keep control of the truck. By this time, the light was red, and cars were crossing in front of me. I had to make a split- second decision, and I steered the truck to the left and headed for my only way out, the grass median. When I had the truck into the grass, I hit the brakes again, and the left front brake locked again. The whole tractor spun around to the left, as I furiously cranked the steering wheel to the right. These types of situations always appear to happen in slow motion. Maybe it was adrenaline or something, I don't know. I was trying to correct the steering, but the tractor spun, clear around and hit the trailer. It hit so hard that my head went through the window and banged off the trailer. I still remember the sound of my head hitting the trailer. After that, I was rolling backwards, and my truck hit a light pole. This impact made my head snap back and break out the back window. The truck finally stopped at the very end of the grass median strip. My first concern was that I didn't hurt anybody. Kenny was shaken up and bruised, but he was OK. I lost my vision in one eye for a minute, but it came back. The whole driver side of the cab was smashed in, and the driver seat was almost over to the passenger seat. I got myself out of the truck and looked around. I had cut it so close that I had peeled off the left side of a Snap On tool truck. He was in the left turn lane, and I had pushed him forward a couple feet and ripped off the sheet metal side. He was OK.

I was just glad nobody was hurt, except me, I guess. The cops arrived, and wrote me up for "failure to maintain proper control", and "defective equipment". A towing company came and took the truck back to the shop in Leesburg. We rode with him and got back home. I was hurt worse than I realized. My arms were sprained from gripping the wheel so tight when we impacted. My head was dizzy. I'm sure I had a concussion, my back hurt, my neck hurt bad, and I was bruised all over. My first reaction was to get a drink. I walked into the bar and said "I need a jack and Coke". They had just opened, and I was drinking really heavy. I explained my situation to the bartender. After about 10 drinks, I went home. Kenny and his wife were asking me if I was OK. I was feeling worse, and they took me to the hospital. The doctors were not very professional and attributed my condition to being drunk. In the coming months, I would deal with severe neck problems, severe pain, amnesia, and back pain. I had to wear a hard collar around my neck, and they got me started on pain pills. I would run into old friends in Fairfax, and I couldn't remember their names. I remember one girl crying when I couldn't remember her name. I took me about six months to recover fully, but I still had neck and back pain.

73 International that I jacknifed. The driver's side of the tractor hit the trailer, and my head broke out the side window.

Then, I was basically rolling backwards into a tool truck and a ditch, and my head took out the back window.

The truck that I hauled air mail in.

The site of my jack-knife accident, with new posts,
and my mudflap still in the ditch.

CHAPTER 26

THE ROUND HILL SHOP

Since the 18 wheeler was totaled, there was no more job with Ahalt Farms. I started working at a fabrication and welding shop in Round Hill, Virginia. Most of the time I would walk to work, along route seven. It was 11 miles, and quite a walk. Almost every day, I would have a new tool or something I had found along the way. Sometimes people would give me a ride. The boss was a great guy, named Floyd, and the other worker was "Squirrel". He was quite a character, and a good friend.

They gave me a job to do, that seemed sort of like an initiation, or a test of my abilities. There was a great big crane truck in front of the shop that had been sitting there for years. I believe it was an International. The engine was out of it, and we went to the machine shop in Herndon, to pick up all the engine parts. When I looked everything over, I could see they were giving us the wrong flywheel. Sure enough, it had gotten switched with another engine. Floyd was impressed that I noticed that. Nobody else did. I brought all the pieces to the shop, and put the engine together. Then I set the engine into the truck with the forklift. In about a weeks' time, I had the whole thing done. When it fired up, and moved, they were impressed. I had resurrected Lazarus from the dead! For me, that was the easy part of the job. Learning to weld and fabricate was new for me. Floyd and Squirrel were good teachers, and I learned a lot.

Round Hill was a small country town, and we would eat lunch at the Town diner, and Floyd would get a few six packs of Miller light after work. I would get another six pack and drink it while I walked home 11 miles. We did a job at the Loudon County Jail, welding bunkbeds into each cell. I may or may not have fabricated a plan, so they could never hold me in there again.

CHAPTER 27

HEY FLOYD, I SCRATCHED UP THE CAR

I guess Floyd felt sorry for me walking to work, so he let me use a 72 Duster. I was in Sterling, after work, and I was helping a friend fix his car. I was driving the Duster with the top box of my rollaway toolbox in the front seat. On the way home that night, I was very tired, and about half wasted. I must have fallen asleep at the wheel, because when I woke up, the car was climbing the embankment on the right side of Route seven. It did a couple of barrel rolls, and landed back on the highway, sliding on its roof. It seemed like it was sliding forever. I was crushed into a tiny space, and I was sliding down the highway upside down. The roof was smashed down to the doors. My toolbox, which weighed a few hundred pounds, had flown up against me on my right side. My right hand was between the steering wheel and the toolbox, which had bent the whole steering column against the left door. My left hand was pinched between the steering wheel and left door. With the roof smashed down on top of me, the car eventually stopped sliding. The roof was red hot! It seemed like I was stuck like this forever, in about a two square-foot space. Finally, an ambulance and fire company came and cut me out with the jaws of life.

They took me to the hospital, even though I told them I was OK. My right hand was swollen from the toolbox hitting it. After checking me out, they released me to a state trooper, who took me to Loudon

County jail. As they were checking me in, I told them I had welded the bunkbeds in. Somehow, I avoided a DUI, and only got charged with drunk in public. I slept in the bed I made that night.

In the morning, I called Squirrel, and he picked me up at the jail, and took me to work. I had to tell the boss, "Hey Floyd, I sort of scratched the car up last night". He was really cool about it. He said he had only paid $200 for it and if I pulled out the engine, he had that sold. Later that day, they brought the Duster in on a flatbed truck. Most tow trucks back then weren't flatbeds, but the car was so destroyed that it had to be on a flatbed. When they saw the car, they both stood there in shock. Floyd said "are you sure you're OK?" I said, yeah, I'm fine. We joked that the front bumper was still good. It was the only piece of the car that survived. This was the first time I saw the car sober, and in the daylight. I had to thank God I was alive! (Again)

While I was still working in Round hill, I put together a 72 Dodge van. My grandfather had passed away and left me 5,000 bucks. When it finally came through, I guess I thought I was rich. I felt bad that I quit my job, because they had been good to me. I was off to the races again, with my cocaine addiction. I would withdraw the daily maximum from the bank, and find a coke dealer. I would get at least a quarter ounce. I had learned the hard way from my second strike, and I fabricated a small cigarette lighter that would hold a gram of coke. The head of the lighter would pop off if it was done right. It would spark if the wheel was turned, but there was no fluid in it. I also had a pack of glass car fuses that I could fill with coke. The lighter passed the drunk in public test when I was arrested in Fairfax. They took it away when I was processed, and then returned it when I was released, the next morning. I was living in the van, and my life was a constant party.

I felt so bad about spending my grandfather's hard earned money, but I couldn't help myself. My grandfather started over 300 diesel mechanic schools, and he wrote the teachers training manual. I hired my friends in the "Six Shooter" band to play at my birthday party. There was a girl who sold large quantities of coke, and I had it at her house. On the way, I stopped at Lynn's house, the friend who talked me out of suicide once. I started putting out lines of coke, and we were talking most of the night. She tried to give me money, but I stuck it in her freezer, where she would find it later. I told her it was cold cash. Anyway, I got to my party when it was about over. I felt like I had done Lynn and her boyfriend a big favor, but looking back, I could've started them into the vicious cycle of addiction. At the party, we were sitting on couches, across from each other. Everybody was a little ticked that I missed most of my own party. They were passing around a Tokemaster bong, with hits of freebase cocaine. The girl across from me was half drunk on wine and had never freebased before. When she took her hit, she vomited clear across the coffee table all over me. I had red fluid dripping down my shirt. She felt so bad about it, but I said, "don't worry it's only wine". I went out to my van to get another shirt. I guess I was looking pretty thin and rough, because the dealer was cutting me off. I had episodes of paranoia, and psychosis from so much coke. I would try to counteract it with alcohol, which helped a little bit. Eventually, the money was gone.

CHAPTER 28

THE DAY I QUIT DRIVING

I was driving the Dodge van on route 123, and I got pulled over. The cop said my license was suspended. Apparently, I owed a parking ticket to Maryland, from my truck driving days. I got all that straightened out, but I never reapplied for my license. I was sick of all the bills that came along with the vehicle, and I couldn't stop drinking, so I stopped driving. The Dodge van went to Bill, because I owed him $250 for Coke. I was walking again.

CHAPTER 29

THE BURKE GARDEN CENTER

My friend Fred worked at the garden center, and got me a job there. I fixed all their equipment, and they let me stay in a storage trailer for a while. I would fix a few things, and get paid maybe 50 bucks. Then I would sit in the trailer, like some kind of hobo, and drink my earnings away. I had a TV set to watch, at least for a while. The shows on TV were an insult to my moral values, and an insult to my intelligence. Shows like Jerry Springer came on, and I only got two channels. I got so offended by the lowlife idiots that America loved to watch, that I kicked the TV clear out of the trailer, onto the parking lot. I was full of alcohol, and full of anger. I was a low life, but at least I had moral values.

I filled in for a mechanic at the Sunoco for a couple days, and then I quit. They were charging people for things that weren't done to the car. After my final day there, I went to a bar on route 236. I had about two beers, and then called a cab, because I was so tired. I waited out front for my cab. I was sitting on the curb, leaning against a brick column, and I fell asleep. I woke up to a Fairfax cop, throwing me across the hood of his car. This woke me right up and kicked in my adrenaline. I started running across the parking lot of the shopping center. He was right on my heels. I crossed a four-lane highway, and he was still on my heels. I went through an apartment complex, and I finally ran out of steam. He tackled me in the apartment complex and arrested me.

I was charged with public drunkenness, and escape of a lawful custody. If I wasn't so tired to begin with, I could have gotten away. This was my second escape charge and about my 20th drunk and in public. I wasn't even drunk. I had a new name pinned on me by the cops. Now they called me "Jackrabbit". On a previous arrest, I was in the back of the cop car, and I had brought my cuffed hands under my feet so my hands were in front of me. Now that really ticked off the cop and he threw me on the ground and re-cuffed me. With my new status of Jack rabbit, the standard procedure was to hog tie me with three sets of handcuffs. They would cuff my hands and feet, and then connect the two with a third set of cuffs behind my back. Then they would throw me in the back seat on my stomach. A drunk in public cost 35 bucks, and didn't require a court appearance. They were becoming routine. I came to work late one day, and Fred said "Didn't I see you in the back of a cop car today?" He was laughing, because he had been down that road too. The boss, Ron, had helped him get into a treatment program, and Fred was doing really well. I had been at a party all night and passed out on the front lawn. Somebody called the cops, and they picked me up off the lawn the next morning. I passed Fred on his way to work. I was on my way to jail. The owner of the garden center was Ron. He was a great guy, and a jokester. After a while, he told me I'd have to find a place to stay besides the storage trailer. There was an abandoned house next-door, and I would sneak in the back door and sleep there. One day the owner came to the front door, and I ran out of the back door. I guess I couldn't stay in the house anymore. There was a small patch of woods between the house and the garden center which became my new home. I guess at least the garden center had a shower. I vividly remember one cold night in the woods there. It was so cold that I snuck in the house and took the old curtains. I rolled myself up in curtains like a cocoon to stay warm. It was freezing, and I can still picture my arm hanging out of the end of the cocoon with a 40 ounce bottle of Budweiser.

CHAPTER 30

SPLITTING HEADACHE

I went to a party at a friend's house. He was a friend of a friend, I guess. I went with my friend, Mike, and I think his friend's name was Cary or something. We were playing quarters with a bottle of whiskey. Cary was apparently dating his first girlfriend, who was getting friendly with me. Cary got jealous and I guess he was drunk. That's all I remember until I woke up in a field next to the patch of woods where I was staying. I couldn't open my eyes, because they were crusted over with blood. I got one eye open and I was covered in blood. I could feel wet blood above my right eye. I was still bleeding. I snuck into the shower at the garden center, but a couple of people saw me covered in blood. I rinsed myself off and changed my clothes. Then I went to the pizza place up the street. The Redskins were playing as I grabbed a beer. A couple of my friends were there and told me I should go to the hospital. I was acting silly and bleeding profusely. I was literally knocked silly. I walked across the street to the fire station, and they immediately put me in an ambulance. It was so bad that a homicide detective showed up, asking me questions at the hospital. They put a bunch of stitches in my head, and ran a lot of tests. I believe this was about my fifth concussion. I would end up with two scars on my forehead, forming an L. The other scar was from the glass exit light that shattered on my head working for A+A. I had the mark of a loser on my forehead. Later that day, I saw Mike at the pizza place, and he told me what happened. Cary had gotten drunk and jealous, and hit me across the forehead with a steel pipe. He said blood went everywhere, and I fell down the steps. Apparently, there was blood all down the stairwell and on the carpet.

Mike had brought me home to the woods, where I lived, but I must have passed out 30 yards from the woods. I relayed this information to the homicide detective, and Mike said he went to the wrong house. It turned out that Cary's family was moving, and that's why he had the party. He had an empty house.

The detective said there was no blood in the house, and I told him to check their old house. They never did.

CHAPTER 31

THE BIRDHOUSE

My friend Mark introduced me to a guy who needed helpers to restore a 100-year- old mansion in Olney, Maryland. It was the home of the late Dr Bird, who founded Montgomery General Hospital. It was a huge three-story house with about 40 rooms, slave quarters, a horse farm with a barn, and a carriage house. There was also a fishing pond and an in ground swimming pool.

The boss was a young guy named Chris, and he was a great person to work for. We had about seven different workers, a plumber, an electrician, etc. I learned a lot from these guys and the work was a nice break from auto and truck mechanic. Every day after work, I would put on my music headphones, and walk up the street to the Olney Alehouse. It was a quaint little bar with great food. They had a six-beer limit, so after a few beers, I would slap on my FM radio headphones, and walk up route 108 to the Cozy Corner. This bar had no limits, and the regulars were more like me. A couple nights, I would be so drunk and tired, walking home, that I would go into a Catholic school that wasn't locked, and I would sleep on the floor for a while. I always woke up before school started, and I may or may not have written some drunken ramblings on the chalkboard. I probably left a faint odor of alcohol in the room too.

Around the time the house was done, my parents came to visit. My dad was impressed by all the work that was done, and he had his case of Budweiser in the trunk. My stepmother was finally on some meds that made her seem almost normal. When she hugged me, it was one of the hardest things I've ever done to hug her back. Forgiveness is a powerful thing, I guess. They say forgiveness is a gift that you give yourself. It's very liberating to let go of hate and anger. It's just a hard pill to swallow.

When the house was done after about six months, they let me stay there as a caretaker. I had the slave quarters all fixed up, and a whole mansion to myself! I would ride the bus to the train, and back on the bus, to work at the garden center in Virginia. Occasionally, I would invite someone from the bar to visit the mansion. They couldn't believe I lived there by myself. The co-owner of the house was named Libby. She had a daughter, Jodi, whose boyfriend played in a heavy-metal band. One night they played at the mansion. I invited a few friends too. It turned into a major party somehow. My friend Warner played for a while. He was an old black man who played some great blues. Jodi's boyfriend Paul's band played too.

There was a cocaine party going on in the attic. The party went all night, and I finally got everyone out. Before I had a chance to clean up, I saw Chris pulling in the driveway. I was so strung out on cocaine, that I didn't want to face him right then. I went out the other way and walked into the woods. I was so quiet, and so on edge, that I walked right up on a deer. I guess it was sleeping, because it jumped up in front of me and scared the hell out of me. I had to face the music the next day, and Chris nicely asked me to move out. He said I should get some help for my drinking, etc. and I understood his point. I moved out.

CHAPTER 32

THE COZY CORNER

I hung out a lot at the bar in Olney, called the Cozy Corner. It was in the corner of the shopping center. I ended up renting a room in a big house with two of the girls who bartended. Michelle, Susan, and me, each paid 400 a month. And I would work in Virginia at the garden center, and then come back to Olney for a while. The bar was owned by a nice lady named Norma, and I did a lot of odd jobs around the bar. I remember one day, a gray fox was running around the shopping center parking lot. Everybody ran out of the bar to check it out. My friend "cowboy" even pulled a Derringer out of his boot to shoot it. I got down on my knees and called the fox. It came right over to me and I petted it. I remember the fur felt wiry and thick. I pointed it to the breezeway in the corner, that led to the woods, and pushed it in that direction. It made it back to the woods, and everybody went back into the bar. They told me I was crazy. Maybe I was, but animals have always seemed to have a connection with me.

There was a very pretty woman who was half drunk, and tried to take me home one night. It was very clear that she wanted to have sex. Her boyfriend was out of town at the time. I used a quote from a Merle Haggard song and said, "I think I'll just stay here and drink." The girls behind the bar were visibly stunned that I turned her down.

Once again, my morals jumped out, probably a good thing. Thinking ahead to when her boyfriend got back. I fixed Cowboy's Bronco, and he would be at the bar every day telling people how good it ran. Pretty soon, I was fixing a Harley Sportster in the garage at the house. I was doing side work in the garage, until Susan claimed the whole garage, so her new boyfriend could park his Harley in there. The roommate situation was slowly unraveling.

CHAPTER 33

BROKEN RIBS

I enjoyed drinking at the cozy corner. There was a whole cast of colorful characters. Terry was the only male bartender, and he could tell jokes for weeks on end, and never tell the same joke twice. He couldn't pronounce his "R's" right, and it made the jokes even funnier. There was Norma, Cindy, Robin, Michelle, Susan, Frank, Cowboy, Eric, and a few others who came in almost every day. Once I heard an argument outback, and I went to check it out. There was a guy and a girl smoking a joint, and the guy was attempting to rape the girl. I jumped in and chased the guy off, and the girl went back in the bar. I can't remember her name, but she would end up helping me out later.

I was riding in a Chevy truck with one of the more rowdy guys from the bar. He was out back, and flying around the back corner of the shopping center. I was drunk myself, and I bailed out of his truck, right before he slammed into the loading dock. I thought I was jumping into the grass along the road. I wasn't expecting to wrap myself around a fire hydrant. I was in bad shape! I was lying there with three broken ribs and I couldn't breathe. It had knocked the wind out of me, and I could barely move. The guy driving the truck had backed up and driven away. Somehow, I crawled to the back door of the cozy corner and banged on the door. Everyone who came out, thought that I was just drunk. I could barely even speak. Finally, the girl who I had helped, listened to me and called me an ambulance. They took me to

Montgomery Hospital, where they told me I had three broken ribs on my left side. There was a lot of other internal damage too. They gave me Percocet, and told me there wasn't much they could do for broken ribs. I couldn't pop that pain pill fast enough. This hurt like hell! It took me a few hours to walk home. Every step was painful!

My roommates were no help at all. If I coughed, which I did quite often from smoking, it would be excruciating! Sneezing was even worse. I had to lay on my bed flat on my back. I tied a sheet to my doorknob to pull myself up out of bed. I couldn't function at all for weeks. Eventually, I could roll myself over to get out of bed. After a couple weeks, I made it back to the bar. The owner, Norma, was mad at me for causing a scene while she had potential buyers at the bar. The rest of my "friends" seemed more intent on buying some of my pain pills. That wasn't happening.

One night, Michelle and Susan asked me if I wanted to go barhopping in DC with them. I said OK, and I rode in Michelle's car to DC. The first bar they went to, all the guys were hitting on them. They were so naïve. There was rap music blasting, and I couldn't stand it much longer. I told them I wanted to leave, but they were too busy enjoying the attention and drinks from the guys. This has bad outcome written all over it. I told them again, "let's leave", but they ignored me. I walked out of the bar in the middle of DC. They would have to deal with the wolves on their own.

I walked through DC, and stopped at the Washington Monument. There were rows and rows of homeless people in sleeping bags under the monument. They offered me a beer, and I accepted, of course. Finally, some real human beings! There were cars pulling up with hot coffee and sandwiches for the homeless people. They gave me a sleeping bag and I went to sleep. In the morning I helped a guy fix his van and he gave me a ride to the garden center. I stayed in Virginia, making money at the garden center for about a week. Since this was before cell phones, I let them wonder if I was OK for a week. They didn't seem to care. While I was gone, a whole bunch of people had moved in. Michelle's mother and father, and a guy named John, who was on methadone. They moved me to the basement, and I wasn't really happy. One night, I got in bed and there was broken glass in my bed, a whole bunch of it. They wanted $400 for rent but when my month was up, I headed across the street into the woods. I set up a little campsite like I had done in Virginia. Now I had $400 in drinking money! Yeehaw!

The radio seemed to play the soundtrack to my life. About this time, "Another Day in Paradise" by Phil Collins, came out. It was about being homeless.

One morning I went into the bar, and somebody asked me what happened to my cheek. I looked in the mirror and I had small deep scratches. I guess it was from a raccoon or something, another blackout from alcohol. There were a few other incidents in Olney. I got punched in the face by a bouncer at the preppy bar. Then I fell flat on my face on the street. Both times I ended up in the hospital with stitches.

Pain pills, alcohol and broken ribs don't mix.

I fixed a car for a girl and her boyfriend from the bar. They had a fight and she ended up hitting a telephone pole. She was seriously hurt and spent a lot of time in the hospital. I made a new policy not to fix cars for people who drink heavy.

Eventually I left Olney and went back to Virginia for good.

CHAPTER 34

BACK TO THE GARDEN CENTER (CINDY)

I was back in Virginia fixing equipment at the garden center. I would work just enough to go out drinking. Sometimes I would get a six pack and sit in the woods by the creek, and drink alone. A girl named Cindy worked there and she asked me if I wanted to go to church. I accepted her offer, and got myself cleaned up for church. It was an event with guitar players, and live Christian music. I had a good time, and met some good people. They had food that was pretty good too.

At the end of the party, each table of about six people had a prayer meeting. Each person said a little prayer out loud. I felt my social anxiety rising. I had no idea what to pray for. One person prayed for their sick family member, while another prayed for this person, or that person. I went last, and I prayed for peace in the world, and to end wars. I also prayed for all those suffering. People seem to look at me funny, as if I were trying to say a bigger or better prayer than they were.

I saw Cindy at the garden center on a Wednesday, three days later. The big news on the TV at the time was that Ronald Reagan had signed a nuclear disarmament agreement the day before, with Mikhail Gorbachev, of the Soviet Union. She smiled a big smile and walked on by. She had to get started working. The Berlin wall fell shortly after that. One of my favorite songs came out by "The Scorpions", called " Winds of change". The band said the song was inspired by thousands of Russians, cheering them on in 1988, when they became the first rock band to play in Russia, and in 1989, at the Moscow music peace festival, even though they were a German band. Being a victim of nuclear testing myself, I felt like God had heard my prayer in a big way. I don't take any credit, it just reinforced my belief in God, even though I felt I was put on this earth to be tortured. I wasn't sure why Cindy had invited me to church. Did she like me? Was she just trying to "save" me? I wasn't sure, so I asked her out on another "date" so to speak. She said she couldn't, and I got the message that she wasn't interested. So much for my love life. I went back to drinking. Jesus drank wine, right? That was one of my justifications. I guess I forgot the part of the Bible that condemns drunkenness.

CHAPTER 35

YELLOW RIVER

I went to a New Year's party in downtown Fairfax, and had a pretty good time. It was a little after midnight when I left. Burke garden center was 6 miles away, and I started walking. I was so tired, and I knew I should get a cab, or I wouldn't make it. I was in a residential neighborhood, and I saw a house where the party was still going on. I knocked on the door, and asked if I could call a cab.

They said they would call me one, and asked me to wait out front. The cab arrived, looking more like a cop car. It took me to jail. As they were processing me, I heard the arresting officer say that I knocked on Officer what's his name's door. They were all laughing.

The cop walked me into a small cubicle and told me to wait there. I told him several times that I had to take a leak. He wouldn't let me use the bathroom, and I was ready to explode. I had been drinking all night. Finally, I had to pick a corner of the cubicle and relieve myself. Nobody noticed right away. They put me in the drunk tank with about six other drunks. I could see a small yellow river moving down the hallway. It must have been a gallon! Shortly after that, they took me to a large cell and about five cops beat the hell out of me. All I could do was roll up in the fetal position. Finally, I heard a woman's voice saying, "we better stop, he's bleeding out of his mouth". They threw me down on the concrete floor and left me there. I was in serious condition. They had re-broken my ribs, which weren't fully healed. All because they wouldn't treat me as a human being, and let me pee.

I could barely walk when I was released in the morning. I was furious! I complained to the magistrate. He sent me to the county building, who then sent me to a lawyer. The lawyer then told me to go to the magistrate. One big circle, and I could barely walk!

You don't have to be black to be a victim of police brutality. Maybe cops should be better educated on dealing with drunk people. I'm sure I said some obnoxious things, but I never touched anybody. They seem to have a limited understanding of mentally ill people too. Fred from the garden center lost his brother Eddie, who was beaten by the cops at a party, and several people saw it. I'm not going to go into detail because I was high myself. Supposedly, he hung himself in jail. Three of Eddie's friends blew up the cops car, while it was parked. They each spent three years in prison. One of these people was Cliff from A+A.

Then there was Roy Buchanan, a famous guitar player. He also had a drinking problem, and he also supposedly hung himself in the Fairfax jail. As a person who visited the drunk tank about 30 times, this seems hard to do. How do you hang yourself after they take all your shoestrings?

And how do you hang yourself in a cell that always has other people in it? They must have moved him to the death cell where they took me. I don't expect any justice here. I've lost all faith in that. It just helps me to forgive when I write about it and let it out. Justice will prevail on judgment day.

I suffered for almost another year, until my ribs fully healed. I had at least 20 bruises where I was kicked and beaten. Maybe cops need anger management training. I've met some good cops too. I try to not be judgmental. It just seemed that I was abused about half the times I was picked up. They even abused my car in California. They got a laugh out of it, I guess.

I fixed a car in West Springfield, Virginia, for a guy that I owned a local bar. I had to put a timing belt on a Dodge Omni, in the shopping center parking lot. I finished the car, and I figured I would sneak it back to Burke, so I could get paid. The car had expired tags, and I had no license since I quit driving. I was looking at the rearview mirror all the way. As I was approaching the red light, I saw a county cop coming up behind me. He was a ways back, so I changed lanes and took a right on red. He turned on the flashing lights and came after me. I did some fancy driving through a subdivision, taking lefts and rights at random. I was hitting 60 to 70 miles an hour, taking turns on two wheels, with tires squealing. When I thought I was in the clear, I drove a few more streets, slowly, and parked the car. I got out and walked to my friend Steve's house. He always had a keg or something, and I cracked open a cold beer, still shaking. I'm not sure he believed me, but I hung out there until the heat was off. I drove the car back and got paid $80. The bar where I got paid was called "Spanky's Clubhouse". it was a small bar in Burke. It reminded me of cheers on TV. There were about 10 regulars. We were all friends, but one day they lost their liquor license. He brought out some O'Doul's nonalcoholic beer, but everybody was out the door. I guess people were there to get drunk, not to socialize.

CHAPTER 36

WESTWOOD

Then there was the coke house on Prosperity Avenue. One of my coke connections lived there. I'll call him Joey, to keep his name confidential. They had a nickname for me, too. They called me Westwood, because I guess I reminded them of Clint Eastwood. They said I should make a cowboy movie or something. I always wore cowboy boots, and I didn't take any crap from anyone. Joey got his coke straight from the cartel in Miami. He would get kilos at a time. I believe they were about $20,000 each. When he wrecked his black Corvette, he got an estimate for $2500. He told me if I could beat that price, he would give me a half ounce for a tip. I priced the parts and they were $1500. I told him $900 Labor which made $2400. He said OK, and I got started. The whole right side of the car was scraped off. He went to give me a half ounce, and I told him, "just give me a couple grams each day, or I'll do the whole bag." So each day he would break me off about a 3 gram rock, and I would take it downstairs to the garage, where I was fixing the car. Upstairs was a 24-hour coke party, and the mirror was always being passed around. There were lots of pretty women, and alcohol. It was hard to get anything done on the car, but I kept working on it. The paranoia and psychosis from too much coke, was creeping in. I taped newspapers over the garage windows so people couldn't look in.

One night, I ran out of coke, and there was no action upstairs, so I took the two front seats out of the car. I had seen him chop up coke on the center console before, and rocks would roll under the seats. I hit the jackpot, picking little rocks of coke out of the back carpet under the seats. Then I put the seats back in real quick before someone saw. Another time I went upstairs in the trash and got the kilo bags and scraped them with a razor blade. I got about a half gram from that.

When I was fixing the car, I noticed that the right fender contained the heating system, but the left fender had a big empty space. I made a stash place that was accessible through the vent in the left kick panel. It would probably hold 10 kg. He thought that was pretty cool. He even asked me if I would make a drug run to Miami. I turned that down.

After about three weeks, the car was finally done. He gave me a big rock of coke as a tip. I was so thin, my ribs were sticking out. I wore a loose shirt to hide it. My pants had to be zip tied around the belt loops to stay up. I had to carry a rag around to wipe blood that was constantly dripping out of my nose. There's a point where the coke doesn't even get you high anymore. I was past that point. I left on good terms, and my mind was made up to quit doing coke. I had some money saved up, and I camped back in the woods with my Budweiser. I thought I had quit drugs, but all I did was substitute alcohol. At least I gained my weight back, and my nose stopped bleeding.

I was staying in the woods by the garden center, and I was going through a severe depression. I believe I had undiagnosed depression to begin with. Add onto that the fact that I had just depleted the dopamine in my brain with massive cocaine use, and top it off with alcohol, which is a depressant. I was cutting my arms, and I didn't know why. The garden center had an outside phone, and I would call my sister Tami in San Diego. I missed her so much. She would be bartending, so I couldn't talk to her long. I was probably annoying to talk to. I was at the end of my rope.

CHAPTER 37

PENNSYLVANIA

Things in Virginia were getting worse. The place was developing everywhere. It was the fastest growing county in the country. There were traffic jams everywhere, and gangs were springing up. My remaining friends were moving west, to get out of the mess. I called my younger sister, Sandy, in Pennsylvania. She came to Virginia and picked me up. She lived in an apartment complex with her husband, Al, and her three kids, Mandy, Emily, and Bobby.

I read a book about alcoholism, and I stayed sober for six months. Then came New Year's Eve, and I walked to a bar at the bowling alley. I thought I had my drinking under control, but I was wrong. After just a few beers, I was plastered. I guess my tolerance was down. I was staggering home, and I got picked up by the Johnstown police. My sister had to come pick me up. It was very embarrassing. My craving for alcohol was back in full force. I was amazed that beers were $.60 apiece in Johnstown. I was used to paying two dollars. I got a place of my own and a job restoring classic cars. The place was called Krieger Classics. The boss's name was Bernie.

Bernie would have me doing several jobs at once. He would take me to his farm and have me fix farm equipment. There was a whole family of Amish workers there. There was the grandfather, the father, and the son. They all dressed the same and I would tell myself they looked like large, medium and small. They were hard workers, and great people. We got to the farm one day, and Bernie says, " Hey, can you fix the hay rake?" I said "Yeah, just show me which one is the hayrake." I started working on it, not realizing that Bernie and another worker were removing one of the big spiked wheels that actually raked the hay. I bent over a steel arm to work on a part, and when they removed the wheel, the arm sprung up with tremendous force. It threw me like a ragdoll, about 40 feet down the gravel driveway. I went over Bernie's truck and his trailer. I landed in the gravel, and everyone was silent. When I got up cussing, and picking gravel out of my skin, they couldn't stop laughing. I didn't think it was all that funny. Of course, I stopped at the first bar on the way home after work. I would always drink till about midnight and go home.

Getting up for work was always torture. Working at Krieger Classics, I had to walk uphill for about 3 miles to work. My head would be pounding, and I felt sick. After about a year there, I quit, or got fired, I'm not sure which. It was a mutual agreement. I would never seem to finish a job, because he would take me from a classic car project to a farm project.

CHAPTER 38

WASTED DAYS

All this time, I was still having neck and back pain from earlier accidents, and moving heavy furniture for 10 years. Pennsylvania had medical assistance for poor people like me. I had been diagnosed by a neurosurgeon, who did MRI scans and all the tests. I had herniated discs in my neck and back. He suggested surgery, but I wasn't real crazy about that. He told me the success rate was 90% and the risks were death, paralysis, impotence, etc. He prescribed me pain pills like Oxycodone, Percocet, and Tylenol number three with codeine. Occasionally, when the pain was bad, I would get a shot of Demerol, which is very dangerous with alcohol. I would usually go straight to the bar and drink.

This would make me extremely impaired, and I would fall down several times walking home. My elbows were always bleeding or healing, and my knees weren't much better. I had a habit of falling off my barstool, and they would just laugh, and drag me off into a corner where I would pass out. I got several more drunk in publics, staggering home every night.

I was evicted from the little house I was renting, for not paying the rent. I started living alongside the highway on a dead-end street, where nobody ever went. I lived between Martin Street and the Johnstown Expressway. I had nothing but a blanket. I stored my tools and things in my sister's shed. I didn't want to stay with her because she had three kids, and I was a mess. I lived there for a few weeks, and then I found out about the Salvation Army. I moved in there, and they helped me apply for low- income housing. I ended up in the projects, called Solomon homes. It was a rough place, with lots of crime. It seemed like a million dollar mansion, after living in the woods again. There were a lot of kids there, who had no father in their life. I would throw the football around with them, and they all liked me.

I grew up with adult role models in my life, and that helped me a lot. I believe in being a role model, and I always loved kids. They cheered me up a lot, and I think I've always been a kid at heart myself. The big, fat slob lady across the hall from me, would leave her smelly bags of garbage in the hallway. It would attract roaches and her apartment was filled with roaches. She had five kids, somehow, and I really felt sorry for her kids. Once she called the cops on me because a kid hugged me. The cops came, and asked all of the little kids if I had touched them inappropriately. They all said no, and the cops checked my records. This made me furious! I didn't play with the kids anymore. I was drunk one night, and had a temper tantrum. I smashed everything in my apartment, and the fat slob called the police again. They came and looked around my apartment, thinking there was a fight. There was nobody there but me.

I was on the third floor of Solomon, in building one, and I would get my drinking money by fixing cars in the parking lot. People knew to bring at least a six pack to get me started. I would carry my heavy toolbox from the third floor, and then back up the stairs again.

CHAPTER 39

THE VICIOUS CYCLE

My normal routine was to fix a car or two, and make some drinking money. Then, I would go on a two or three-day drinking binge, til the money was gone. I didn't steal or commit crimes for drug and alcohol money, like a lot of people around me. My medical card paid for my pain pills. When the money was gone, I would lay in bed and detox for a few days. I would have night terrors that were horrific! I would dream of snakes, all around me that were as big as telephone poles. And there were dreams of packs of dogs chewing me up, or bugs crawling all over me. The only way to get rid of the bugs was to drink again. Anyway, after the brutal detox phase, I would eat some soup, and eventually some food. I believe that eating once a week probably saved my liver, and my life. Then I would fix a few cars in the parking lot, and go on another binge. It was a weekly vicious cycle. I was slowly dying, in a downward spiral.

CHAPTER 40

CAMBRIA COUNTY PRISON

I was making payments on a drunk in public charge, and I missed a few payments. The magistrate sent out a couple of his constables to pick me up. They went to Hollern's bar, but they had just missed me. My friend, Erin, was a bartender there, and she told them I had a few beers and left. She said I might be at Charlotte's Web, the next bar, about a mile away. The constables went to Charlotte's, but I had just left there too. Then they went to the clubhouse, and I had just left there too. They finally caught up with me at the Lonestar hotel. They cuffed me, and took me to the magistrate. He asked me if I had $300, and I didn't so he threw me in the old Cambria County Prison. It was the creepiest thing I've ever experienced. It is a Gothic revival style building, built in 1872. It's supposedly haunted, and was featured on "Destination Fear". It has a dungeon in the basement, with shackles on the walls. There used to be gallows outside, where people were hung. Inside, there's a series of cell blocks that look like a big cage, inside of the four walls. They would bring in prisoners screaming, and it would echo throughout the building. I was put in a cell with a crazy Jamaican drug dealer. He would dance around the little cell, to the music in his little radio. I just held a pillow over my ears. When everybody got a one-hour recreation break, I would just stay in my cell to get one hour of peace and quiet. I had learned a long time ago, how to tune out my surroundings, and go to another place in my mind. I believe it was a defense mechanism I developed, to keep from losing my sanity. Kind of like the James Taylor song "Going to Carolina in my mind." I had definitely seen "Fire and Rain" in my life.

After 13 days and 14 nights in this living hell, they told me I was getting out. The prison was in Ebensburg, and they gave me a bus token to get to Johnstown. As I walked out the front door, I saw sunlight again, and there was a nice church across the street. I walked to the bus stop, and hopped on a bus to Johnstown. I grabbed the first beer I could get my hands on, and it sure tasted good. I was back to my old habits. I was free at last, but still a prisoner of my addictions.

CHAPTER 41

ROCK BOTTOM

There were several more bad luck injuries, etc. and I was at an all-time low. It's hard to put into words what it felt like, to be completely hopeless, spiritually dead inside, physically almost dead, and completely depressed. My solution at the time was a depressant, alcohol. I was cutting my arms, I guess to feel something besides nothing.

I had a friend named Barb, who also was addicted to pain pills. She was really worried about legal charges she had, for forging a prescription. She would never appear in court because she froze to death in her car. Another friend of mine hung herself in the projects.

I was picked up off a sidewalk in Dale Borough, by some paramedics one night, I guess my body temperature was really cold, and I was bleeding from my mouth. I was becoming a regular passenger in the ambulance. This time, though, the paramedics seemed worried. The doctor told me I was literally dying. I didn't really care. It would be an end to all this torture. I remember talking to my sister, Sandy, with tears in my eyes. She suggested that I get treatment, which I had never considered. I didn't think it would work.

She told me that she did some checking, and my medical card would cover everything. All I had to do was show up. I thought a rehab would cost $30,000, like it did in Virginia. I had tried 1,000 ways to quit, and nothing ever worked. I decided to take a leap of faith and give it a shot.

CHAPTER 42

GOODBYE PARTY

I went to a morning assessment, at a program called "New Visions." I talked to a nice lady named Michelle. She asked me if I had drunk any alcohol that morning, and I said "yeah." I guess she thought I was in really bad shape, because she wanted me to be admitted immediately. This was on a Monday, and I told her I would check in on Wednesday, because I have my friend's car all apart, and I needed to finish it. She probably thought I was chickening out, but I was serious.

I finished a head gasket job on a Shelby Daytona, turbo, for my friend Brett. Then I delivered it to him and got paid. I decided to catch one last buzz for some reason. Brett and I smoked weed, drank pitchers of beer, and played pool at the bar.

I should've been feeling pretty good at this point, but all I felt was sick. I had a routine, as a bar room maintenance man, for about five bars, all in a row across town. I would get free beers, and shoot pool at the last bar, for a beer a game. I drank all day for free, on most days. I would do everything from cleaning greasy fryers, to fixing toilets.

Anyway, this was my last time in a bar for quite a while. I told people I was quitting, and they laughed. I couldn't blame them. The bar crowd treated me very badly, and very disrespectfully. I made a vow to myself right there and then, that I was going to show them!. I guess anger was one of my motivators at the time.

I drank til late that night, bought a few packs of cigarettes, and walked to the hospital to check in. It was Tuesday night, and I didn't even feel buzzed at all. I just felt very sick. The detox unit was right next to the morgue, at Conemaugh hospital. I remember going through the double doors and checking in. At the end of this hallway, there's a spot where I could touch all three doors. The left door was the morgue. The morgue had a real funky smell. The right door was the AA meeting room. Straight ahead was the detox unit. They gave me some kind of pill to help me detox. My blood alcohol content was .25, and I felt normal. The doctors did a physical assessment, and I ended up with IV tubes, hoses, and wires attached to me. I was almost dead.

CHAPTER 43

CHECKING MYSELF IN

It was Wednesday morning, and I woke up in the detox. I had tubes and wires hanging off of me. I was lying in a hospital bed, wearing hospital pajamas. There was a small room off the detox unit, where they let me smoke a cigarette. I was shaking so bad, that it was hard to hold the flame, to light the cigarette. They told me to attend the morning AA meeting, which was the first door down the hall. I walked in, rolling my IV poles along with me, wearing pajamas and all. There were about 30 people at the meeting, sitting in a circle. I must've been a sight to see, 60 pounds underweight, shaking, pale, and sickly looking. I thought people were looking down on me, but they were probably praying for me, silently, and thinking that they could very easily be in the same situation. A girl said hi to me, and I didn't recognize her at first. Then it hit me. It was my friend Candi. She had been out drinking with me a few times. She drank me under the table, literally. She would do a shot with every beer, and I was only drinking beer. She would be headed to the next bar, and I would be staggering home.

I didn't recognize Candi at first, because she looked completely different. She had gained her normal weight back, and looked beautiful! She was six months sober. She really inspired me that day, and I felt that maybe I could do this! I got my 24 hour coin at the meeting, and they told me, "one day at a time". I could even break it down to one hour, or one minute at a time. The first three days were brutal! It was one minute at a time.

A woman named Tammy was my caseworker. She did all the paperwork to get me into rehab. I was pleasantly surprised that nobody had been judgmental, when everybody treated me with respect. I spent three rough days in the detox unit. I went to the morning meeting each day. I didn't say much, due to my frazzled nerves, and my social anxiety.

On the fourth day, a guy named Mike came and picked me up for rehab. I asked if I could bring a guitar, and he said OK. We picked up a small amp and guitar at my apartment, and went off to his rehab in Cresson, Pennsylvania. I believe his wife Gail was a co-owner, and the place was called Cedar Manor.

It was an all-male facility, with a senior citizen facility upstairs. There was a smoking area outside. My sister brought me a carton of generic cigarettes. They cut all sugar and caffeine out of our diet, and we would go to Nautilus fitness center every day. I would try to do one pull up on the bar, and I couldn't. A far cry from setting my high school record, with 20 something pull-ups. I would exercise a little bit though, and I always felt a little better afterwards.

Two weeks into the rehab, I went into shock from withdrawal, and serious neck and back pain. They took me by ambulance back to the Conemaugh hospital, in Johnstown. Since so many doctors don't understand addiction, there was a special doctor named Dr. Pote. He gave me a non-narcotic pain shot, and Toradol for pain.

Then they released me.

I walked out of Conemaugh hospital, looking out onto Franklin Street. To my right, I could see the neon lights of Murphy's, the Haven, and all the other bars down the street. They were trying to call my name. To my left was a row of payphones. I called Mike at Cedar Manor, and he came and got me. He even got me a carton of generic cigs.

Moments like that probably saved my life! He didn't have to drive 25 miles to Johnstown, late at night to get me. He didn't have to lend me 10 bucks for cigs. I am eternally grateful for Mike!

Back at the rehab, I was feeling a little better. We had classes that lasted 50 minutes, with 10-minute cigarette breaks in between. I learned a lot from the three counselors who did the classes. We would visit AA meetings at night, and I picked up a lot of knowledge there too. We would all sit around a dinner table, and they fed us very well. Each of us had a designated chore to do.

We had an exercise to calculate how much money we spent in our addictions. I calculated a five-year period out of 27 years of drugs and alcohol. Working for A+A, I made about $400 a week for driving and moving, and another weekly check for about $300, for fixing trucks. That's $700 a week, which was good money at the time. I multiplied $700 a week times 52 weeks in a year, times five years. I had spent $182,000 in just five years, of my 27 years of drug and alcohol use. It started to make sense why people my age had big houses, and I didn't. I had paid for the entire legal system to buy a house.

We did a few fun things at rehab, and I had beaten everybody at horseshoes, scrabble, basketball, etc. I lost at ping pong. I got sharked. I was sitting outside in the smoking area, and one of the counselors, Bill, sat down next to me. He asked me about the scars on my arms. I told him they were from being drunk, depressed, and hopeless. He asked me why I came to rehab, and I told him I wanted to get sober and clean. He asked which court had sent me here. I said, "I came here on my own." He replied, "Well, we'll find out anyway." It was like being called a liar. I guess most of the addicts had become liars, but I seldom told a lie. I lied to myself, mainly, telling myself I didn't have a problem. When you're staring death in the face, the lie doesn't fly. I had a big problem. I did a lot of things for the first time. I realized that I had a problem. I realized I couldn't stop without help. I asked for help for the first time. I checked myself into a controlled environment, where I was safe from myself for a month. A couple guys couldn't make it through the withdrawal and they called a friend for a ride out of there. I was hanging in there, biting the bullet.

We would be riding in the big van, and we would be goofing off sometimes. We would pass a place called "mainline pharmacy" and half the guys would say "Hey, drop me off here". We called the van "the druggie buggie "or the "dope fiend limousine". The big treat was a coffee on the way.

I remember distinctly, when I knew was going to survive this. I was riding in the druggie buggy, just looking out the window. I think my spirit awoke or something, but it was a shining ray of hope. A spiritual person would call this a spiritual awakening. A neurosurgeon would say that the dopamine, serotonin, etc. were starting to flow again. Whatever it was, I liked it, and I wanted more of it. This was a natural high. I hadn't felt this in a very long time. There was a great person emerging from under all the drugs and alcohol.

It was a great day when I graduated from rehab, and I got my red 30 day coin! I hadn't been sober this long in years. I knew my life depended on me staying clean and sober. I was getting regular blood tests, to see if my liver would get better or worse.

CHAPTER 44

A NEW CHANCE AT LIFE

They drove me back to Johnstown from the rehab, and I felt like a new man. I told them to drop me off at the 8 pm AA meeting. There were about 30 regulars at the meeting, and an occasional newcomer. They told me I looked a lot better, without the IV poles and the pajamas. I was putting the tools I learned to use.

Here are the tools I used:

1. A higher power of my choice. I chose Jesus Christ. I felt he knew what it was like to suffer greatly.
2. Don't use ANY drugs or alcohol.
3. Avoid stress, the number one cause of relapse.
4. Get a sponsor.
5. Go to meetings, establish a support group.
6. Change my people, places, and things. (The only thing I had to change was everything.)
7. Work the 12 steps.
8. The three spiritual principles (H.O.W.) Honestly, Open mindedness, and Willingness

After the meeting, I went back home to my apartment in the projects. There was an eviction notice on my door, and the apartment smelled like empty beer cans. I opened my closet door, and an avalanche of empty beer cans came down. I had to clean the whole apartment, and I even took the beer posters off the walls. I had the bright idea to put all the papers from past consequences into a book bag, to remind me of what drinking and drugging was really like. The bag was completely full, with 31 drunk in publics, 2 escapes, multiple hospital bills, and a whole variety of bad experiences.

I had to resolve my eviction notice with the Johnstown Housing Authority, and I began to clean up the consequences of my addictions, one at a time. Three guys from my rehab actually lived in the neighborhood. They all went back to drinking and drugging.

I took my recovery very seriously. I was waiting for the bus one day, and my old drinking buddy, Frank, drove up. He said he would take me downtown, but he went straight down Solomon Run road, instead of turning left. About this time, I smelled alcohol on him, and I realized he was half drunk. He said we were going to the Country Inn, and I said I wasn't going. I explained that I had just been in rehab for 30 days, but he didn't seem to care. He said "Just drink a soda", and I said no again. I said no one more time, before I reached between the front seats and yanked up on the parking brake handle. The car skidded a little sideways to a stop, and I got out. I guess he didn't realize how serious I was. I walked back to the bus stop, and he headed to the bar.

My old drinking buddies were coming around a lot. I answered my door at my third-floor apartment, and it would be one after another. They all seem to say the same thing, "let's go to the bar "or "hey I just got a six-pack". I learned how hard it was to reason with a drunk person.

CHAPTER 45

BOUNDARIES

My caseworker explained to me in detox how they would schedule my recovery process. After detox and rehab, I would attend outpatient counseling for 18 weeks. Most of the group members didn't want to be there, but I loved going to group. I found a shortcut to the hospital where they had "New Visions." I would walk from the projects down Messenger Street, and across the train bridge to the hospital. I would be looking down between the railroad ties at the river below. It was a little scary to look down. There were three sessions a week, two groups, and one individual session. My individual counselor was Mark, and my group counselor was Jeff. There was a lady named Barb, and Michelle, who did my initial assessment.

I would unload my problems on Mark at my individual session. He taught me about setting boundaries, which was a whole new concept to me. I was so used to being a people pleaser, it was nice to know that I didn't have to make everyone like me. My first boundary was the door of my apartment. I didn't have to answer it, when my old drinking buddies came knocking. I would look out the peep hole, and see who it was. Another boundary was the front door of every bar in town. I was walking by Hollern's Tavern, and my friend Erin said hi, and invited me in. I pointed to the line under the door and told her, "I can't cross that line." She understood, and supported my recovery. It seemed like when I was drinking, and I needed alcohol so badly, no one ever had any. But since I've been sober, everybody was putting alcohol in my face. It was as if Satan was tempting me repeatedly. I was riding my 10-speed bicycle around with my FM headphones on, and saw my friend Kelly. She's a good-looking redhead, and I almost hit a light pole. I rode up to her, and she said she wanted to go to the bar. I thought about it, but then I said I couldn't. This disease of addiction was attacking all of my weaknesses.

I was riding down Ohio Street on a Tuesday night, on my bike, and I heard music coming from the Ohio Street lounge. Then I realized it was an open mic night on Tuesdays, and there was a party going on. I had played guitar there before on open mic night. I had to be half drunk to get up in front of the audience. I started thinking about all the pretty girls that were usually there. I was sitting on my bicycle with a wrestling match going on in my brain. I put my headphones on, and rode away. I was feeling really good, and sometimes I would ride into Coney Island restaurant, around 2 AM. All the people were coming from the bars and I couldn't believe how ridiculous they acted. That was me just a short time ago. I was actually worse than them.

I was listening to some cassette tapes of me and my friend George playing guitar. We must have left the tape recorder running, even after the song. I could hear myself talking, and I must have been drunk when we recorded it. Was that really me? It was! That was enough to keep me sober another day.

When I worked on a car, I would put a can of Pepsi where I used to put a can of beer. Sometimes, I would get a glass of ice cubes and cherry Pepsi. It was my substitute for Jack and Coke. I was playing mind games with my own mind.

The first car I fixed sober, I made $40. Both bills were series 1950, and they had my name on them! (Robert Anderson, secretary of the treasury)

The first car I fixed sober, I made $40.

Both bills were series 1950 and had my name on them!

(Robert Anderson, secretary of the treasury.)

The other miracle is that they never got spent. I still have them!

I noticed something else while riding around on my bike. I was actually being more careful, in dangerous situations where I would've been reckless before. I was starting to care about myself. I was starting to like myself. One of my biggest problems before this, was that I didn't care about myself.

I couldn't even look at my guitar for a few weeks, after getting home. I never played it before without drugs or alcohol. After a while, I picked it up, and enjoyed playing. I would actually remember what I learned the day before. One of my favorite guitarists, Stevie Ray Vaughan, had gotten sober for three years before he died in a helicopter crash. I read a book called, "Caught in the crossfire", about him, and it inspired me.

I also noticed that I was picking up where I went off track, 27 years ago. I was dealing with social anxiety, head-on, instead of drinking for courage. I was building model cars from Walmart, like I had long ago. I was working through the grief of losing my mother, without drowning my sorrows. They say people don't mature in addiction because they don't work through the struggles of life. They run away from them.

I would go to the AA meeting every morning, and a lot of the night meetings. Some people call AA a cult, or other names. The truth is that it's just a bunch of people trying to stay sober. Everyone is free to choose their own higher power, or even no higher power, if they choose. They are self-supporting through their own contributions. I learned a lot of valuable life skills through AA, NA, counseling, etc. They should teach us that stuff in schools.

When I hung out with my drinking buddies, all I would hear is "let's go drinking". At AA, I heard 30 people talking about NOT drinking. If I started my day with a meeting, I would have almost no cravings that day. I had a strategy of fixing one problem each day. There was a mountain of consequences to resolve. It was overwhelming, if I looked at the whole mountain. I started with the eviction notice. I went to the housing authority, and explained my situation, with a letter from the rehab. They let me stay. Then, I had two drunk in public charges to pay, at two different magistrates. I didn't want to revisit the "Stone Hotel". I sold my favorite guitar, and paid both fines in full. I was buying peace of mind.

I owed my sister 50 bucks, and I paid her back. One by one, I was cleaning up the mess. The mountain of junk was getting smaller, and eventually it was gone. I wasn't creating new problems either. I was feeling good about myself, and people told me I looked much better.

At the meetings, I didn't say much. My social anxiety was through the roof. My hands would sweat big puddles on the table. My stomach would even growl. The coffee would make me even more nervous. I felt better if I talked though, so I talked with a shaky voice.

I had some issues with anger, and my counselor helped me work through it. I would fix a car for somebody, and they wouldn't pay me. This made me angry and anger made me want to drink. My counselor told me it's OK to say no to people. He suggested I get payment upfront or other methods. I felt like I was being a jerk, but I was proud to be standing up for myself for a change. I stopped being a doormat for people to walk all over. I was too nice to people and too trusting. I was also too sensitive to emotional pain. I had so much to work on! As long as I didn't pick up the first drink or a drug, I could work through all of my issues.

I had a good friend named Casey, who lived across the street from my apartment in the projects. She was very helpful in my recovery.

When I dropped all my drinking friends, I had one friend left, Casey. She ended up getting married, and moved to New York. She rented me her house, and I was finally out of the projects. I would look out the window and see my old drinking buddies knocking on the door of my old apartment across the street.

I went to the music store, Music Haven, for some guitar strings, and Ray, the owner, asked me if I wanted to clean out their attic. I looked upstairs, and I immediately said yes. Since I didn't have a driver's license yet, my sister and I rented a U-Haul truck. I loaded up six organs, 25 guitar cases, about 25 broken guitars, speakers, mixers, etc. On the same day I sold 25 guitar cases for 10 bucks each to my friend Don. The U-Haul was 40 bucks, so I made 210 bucks on the first day! I started a new hobby repairing guitars. Don taught me a lot about that. He was 70 something, and he was rated among the top 10 steel guitar players in America. I found a great big wooden desk unit, and I made a guitar workbench out of it. It had previously been the admitting desk at the maternity ward of Lee hospital. I had to cut 4 inches from the bottom of it, to get it in the house.

I was back at Music Haven, and they said "Hey, put your name in this box, and you could win a brand new Fender Stratocaster". They didn't have to ask me twice!

CHAPTER 46

MY LUCK CHANGES

I fixed a couple of broken guitars, and my neighbor's daughter wanted one. She didn't have any money, so I gave her a nice guitar. The following Saturday was the drawing at music Haven. There were about 40 people standing in a circle in the parking lot. You had to be at the drawing to win the guitar, so I was figuring my odds were about 40 to 1. They had a small boy, about five years old, stick his hand in the box and pull out a name. They called my name, and I about fell over! I had just won a 97 Fender Stratocaster! It was as if I had ordered it the way I wanted it. It was candy apple red, with a maple neck, and vintage hardware. It was made in the US too. It was called the "California Strat".

L to R, Ray, me, and Casey

I was so happy, I had a sudden urge to celebrate. I wanted to drink really bad, but I didn't. I went to a meeting and talked about it. After identifying the triggers that made me want to drink, this was a new one. Being happy was a whole new feeling. For that matter, everything was new and different. Where people used to steal from me, now people were giving me things. Casey gave me a nice leather jacket. Where I used to have bad luck, and bad things happening, now I had good luck and good things happening. I suddenly realized that 90% of my problems were coming from drugs and alcohol.

I remember being afraid to go to rehab, and then being afraid to get out. Going into rehab was scary, because I thought life would suck without drugs and alcohol, and I was scared of withdrawal symptoms. When I got out of rehab, I was scared of relapsing, and afraid of change. My counselor Jeff told me that my turning point was when my fear of death became greater than my fear of change. I thought it was ironic, that when I sold my favorite guitar to pay for my fines and I gave away a guitar, I ended up winning a new guitar that was worth three times as much as both of them.

Whenever I made a lot of money fixing a car, I would reinvest it in myself. I bought air tools to make work easier. A lot of money in my pocket could be a trigger. They taught me in rehab that it would be like the devil on one shoulder, talking in your ear, and an angel on the other shoulder, telling you the right thing to do. The devil must've tempted me 1000 times, and I had several ways to deal with cravings. First, I would recognize that my disease was talking to me, and then I would stop what I was doing, and say the serenity prayer, or call my sponsor, Chris. Or I would think of something like the Cambria county prison or something. They call it euphoric recall, when the devil on my shoulder reminded me of the good times I had drinking, but never the bad times. I had already proven to myself on my last day of drinking, that it wasn't fun anymore. They taught me the four stages of a craving. One, the trigger. It was unavoidable. Two, the thought, I would use the process of thought stopping instead of entertaining the thought. If I entertained the thought too long, it goes to stage three, the craving. Four is the relapse. Relapse wasn't an option. My life depended on me not relapsing. I came close a couple times.

CHAPTER 47

CLOSE CALLS

I went to the meeting one morning, and a girl from the halfway house was talking about her struggles. A guy who thought he was some kind of AA guru was telling her what she should do. The rules of AA are, there are no advice givers, or counselors. Everyone is free to recover at their own pace. People were arguing, and the whole meeting ticked me off. A newcomer walked out the door. I left there in a bad mood, and then some other things made me mad. I felt like getting drunk really bad. I did everything I could think of, to not drink. I walked around town because walking helped me think straight. I even went to the 12-noon mass, at St. John Gaulbert. Finally, I felt better. It was like the disease was starving inside me, and it was Screaming, "feed me!"

Meanwhile, I was living in the little white house that I rented from Casey. I inherited two dogs with the house. There was Two-tone, a small, brown and black dog, and there was Max, a big hairy dog. I'm not sure what breeds they were. When I reached one year sober, I applied for my driver's license. I was terrified that my past offenses would come back to haunt me, but they didn't. I fixed up a Chevy van that I bought from a plumber. I had to catch him between his drinking binges, to sign the title over. When I was cleaning the van out, I had a small campfire going. I reached way up under the front seat, and a full can of beer rolled out, practically touching my nose. It was a 16-ounce Budweiser, just like I used to drink. At first, I thought I should throw

it in the fire. Then I thought I better empty it first. I popped the top
and threw it in the fire. I was triggered three times in three seconds!
First, by the sight of it, right in my face. Second, by the sound of the
top popping, and third, by the smell of it. I threw it in the fire without entertaining the thought of drinking it. My disease tried a triple
whammy on me, but it didn't work. I was beginning to understand
why they call the disease cunning, baffling, and powerful.

Then there was New Year's Eve, and my next-door neighbor insisted that I do a shot of whiskey. I had to insist that he take his drunk
ass back in the house. He said, "Wow, you've really changed" in an
insulting tone of voice. I said "thank you." I was working on the van,
out in front of the house one day, and I wasn't in a good state of mind
that day. I somehow decided I wanted to go to the bar. I went to get
the keys from the front porch, and they were gone. Everything else was
right where I left it. My soda, cigarettes, everything but my van keys.
Two tone was sitting there, looking at me funny. I had a feeling she
had taken my keys. I wouldn't find them until 2 AM when all the bars
were closed. They were in the backyard. Very strange!

CHAPTER 48

TITHING

I worked on a ladies Cavalier a few times, and she was a great customer. She was referred to me by a friend. She called me one day, and told me she does a tithing thing once a year. I had never heard of this, but she explained that it's like a donation. She said that this year, God told her to give me 100 bucks. I told her she must have a direct line to God, because I was 100 short on making my rent this month. I told her I would do some work on her car to repay her, but she said no, she didn't want any repayment. There were other occurrences that were way beyond coincidence. I could understand 40 to 1 odds of winning the guitar, but there was something, magical or spiritual going on here. It was like I had guardian angels, and they were rejoicing, because the prodigal son had finally come home. Maybe my mom in heaven was looking out for me.

I was still getting blood tests every month, and luckily, my liver was healing slowly, and my blood counts were improving. Looks like I'm going to survive!

There were some sad things that happened too. I ran into Candi, who had been doing so good, and she looked terrible. She looked 30 years older! She had relapsed, and she passed away shortly after that. I think she was 30 something. I began to understand why they talk so much about feelings in rehab. My feelings were off the charts! I had gone from feeling nothing, to feeling everything intensified.

My biggest problem was chronic pain, from 15 car accidents. I took naproxen to take the edge off the pain. I'll leave out most of the car accidents, but it's amazing that I survived some of them. Thank God I didn't hurt or kill anybody!

I even had some OCD symptoms that I never had before. I would check my door locks, my coffee pot, and other things constantly. Everything had to be in its place, and nothing crooked. I had a fear of heights, that I never had before. I had to face all these fears to overcome them. I had dreams that I relapsed, and I would wake up sweating and shaking. I learned to actually fight back in my dreams when something, or someone, was attacking me. After that, most of the bad dreams went away. The OCD slowly went away too. It was a daily struggle.

Early recovery can be really hard. Later in recovery, it can seem too easy. A lot of my friends thought they were cured after six months, or a year. I tried to take suggestions, which were based on a lot of people's failures, and practiced what I was taught. Complacency is when the disease says. "Go ahead, you can have one beer, you deserve it". I was now in the maintenance stage.

CHAPTER 49

STEP 5

I worked on the 12 steps as best I could, doing some things out of order. For instance, I made some amends right off the bat, to clear my conscience. I paid back my sister, etc. I eventually came to step five, which says "Admitted to God, to ourselves, and another human being, the exact nature of our wrongs." I figured that going to confession at church would be a good way to do it. I stepped into the little booth, and said, "Bless me, father, for I have sinned, it has been 27 years since my last confession!" I explained to him that I was finally sober. My penance was to take a monthly missalette from the church's pews, and read the readings every Sunday before church. Then, I was supposed to attend church every Sunday for eight weeks. When I left confession, I felt like a heavy weight had been lifted off my back. I attended church for eight weeks, and that helped me a lot too. In my recovery, I found it was easier if I used every single tool of recovery. I attacked the disease and surrendered at the same time. The surrender was admitting to myself, that I could never drink or drug successfully. I had already tried every form of moderation, substitution, etc., and nothing ever worked. I thought of never taking the first sip, because I never really liked the taste of alcohol, until I was half drunk. Recovery was hard, but addiction is harder. Recovery always gets better. Addiction always gets worse.

CHAPTER 50

MY FIRST MEETING

I went to one AA meeting, and the topic was "our first AA meeting." I talked about being in Virginia, and hurting my knee really bad. I was jumping over a wall, between two bars. I crawled into the bar and ordered a beer and an ambulance. They took me to Fairfax Hospital, and my knee was purple from internal bleeding. The doctor fixed me up, and arranged for a cab for me. They insisted that the cab driver drop me off at the local AA meeting. I guess they were tired of seeing me in the ER, smelling like a brewery.

At the meeting, I hobbled on my crutches to a chair in a big circle. A lot of people welcomed me, and I asked how the meetings work. They told me when it comes around the circle to me, that I should say "Hi, I'm Bob, I'm an alcoholic." I said, what if I'm not an alcoholic? To me, an alcoholic was a guy who lived under a bridge with a brown paper bag. They said, "Just say, I'm Bob, I have a problem with alcohol".

When I said that, everybody laughed. If I had been honest with myself at the time, I would've realized, hey, at least an alcoholic has a bridge. I have been homeless in three states, and I never had a bridge to keep me dry. I also didn't know at the time that alcoholism is a brain disease. I condemned the whole meeting because of what one person said. They said they were selling pot to pay for their rent. I got a ride home from a guy who was trying to help me, but I wasn't ready yet. I would suffer for about 10 more years before I was ready to change.

I was in denial. I honestly believed in my mind that I didn't have a problem. That's the insanity of addiction. I would have to reach a point where I was staring death in the face, to admit to myself that I had a problem.

CHAPTER 51

TWIN LAKES

It was during 2002, when I was attending the morning AA meeting, when I first met the adolescents from the Twin Lakes rehab, in Somerset Pennsylvania. They would come to the Johnstown meeting in a van. I had six years clean and sober, and I was a whole new person. I saw myself in these kids, who had been through a lot. Some of the older members of AA would tell them what they should do, and look down on them for drug use. They would say things like, "When I was your age," or treat them like they didn't belong, because the older guys were against drugs, and thought they were somehow worse than alcohol. The supervisor for the kids asked me if I would come to their rehab, and speak to the kids. I still had a lot of social anxiety, and I asked her how many people would be there. She said 15 or 20, so I gathered up my courage and said yes.

My first trip to Somerset went very well. I told my story as the kids listened intently. They all thanked me for coming and told me to come back again, and bring my guitar.

Please come Sept 8, 2002

RULES FOR CLUB DOWN UNDER

GUEST SPEAKER

Bob,

We would like to thank you for your support of Twin Lakes Adolescent Program.

It is very important to help make a difference in the life of our youth. Especially youth that are battling drug and alcohol addictions.

It is an unselfish act to come and share your time with our adolescents with words of encouragement, hope, and steps toward recovery.

Our facility is a structured environment and also a smoke-free environment. Therefore we ask that you please adhere to the following suggestions before you arrive to speak.

❖ **Please leave your purse in your car or allow us to secure it while you are speaking.**
❖ **Please do not bring any tobacco products into the facility nor give any of the tobacco products to the adolescents.**
❖ **Please do not give the adolescents your personal telephone number or address.**

We ask that you understand the importance of these simple yet necessary rules in conjunction with their treatment.

Thank you for sharing something that can never be replaced, and that is your Time! Again we thank you.

IN CLOSING   *WHAT YOU SEE HERE*
                      WHAT YOU SAY HERE
                      WHEN YOU LEAVE HERE
                      LET IT STAY HERE

Thank you so much for giving so freely your time to the kids

Twin Lakes Center
Adolescent Unit Staff

443-3639

My second time there, I brought my guitar and amp. They had a fun day at a place in Somerset, called the Club Down Under. It was down some steps, under another business. It used to be a bar, so it triggered me a little. There were pool tables, etc. I played some music, and then we all sat down and had a little recovery meeting. I was struck by how honest these kids were. I told them, well, you've heard about me, now I'd like to hear about your stories. Some of their stories were heartbreaking, and one girl's story brought tears to my eyes. I learned right then, that it was more important for me to listen, than to talk. These kids were unloading their problems like I had in my rehab. I never told them what they should do, but I told them what had helped me when I was in the same situation. In a lot of ways, I was still a kid myself.

I ended up starting a Monday night NA meeting for them, in a little stone building on the rehab property. Every Monday, I made the trip from Johnstown to Somerset. I loved that meeting, and it gave me a sense of purpose, and did wonders for my self-esteem.

The kids would make me thank you cards, and they are still my favorite possession. Some were very artistic, and some were stick figures. I loved them all. I have a big stack of them. I even donated an acoustic guitar that I fixed up. They were impressed that I remembered their names so well, but I must admit, I cheated a little bit, because my memory was still bad. I would get there a little early, and look at their chore sheet on the wall. Then I would refresh my memory of their names. When the meeting started, some of them wouldn't be happy. When it ended, they would tell me they felt a lot better. I would usually start the meeting with a topic of "today". Then I told them I got this far by taking it "one day at a time", and asked them how today was going for them. They would complain about this or that, but then they would feel better. They would resolve issues between each other. Then I would ask them to pick another topic. They didn't have to speak if they didn't want to. I never had kids, and these kids changed me. I think they helped me more than I helped them. A lot of them would come to my meeting, even after they were discharged. The Twin Lakes management didn't want to pay for any supplies, such as books, tokens, etc., so I bought them myself. I made my own tokens for one day, one month, two months, etc. They were made of colored aluminum coins from the locksmith shop, and I had them engraved at the trophy shop. I bought books and other supplies at the NA regional meeting, which was every third Saturday in Ebensburg. The regional chairman was kind of a jerk. He called me the NA renegade, because my meeting wasn't sanctioned by NA. He told me that "Hospitals and institutions" had certain rules that I wasn't following. He was just mad because he spoke at Twin Lakes, and brought a whole entourage of people, and they didn't want him to come back. Anyway, I had to sit through their debate, about paying $.12 per meeting schedule. I think I embarrassed them all, because they were arguing over $.12 paper schedules, and I slapped down 150 bucks for books, tokens, and other things for the kids. I told them I spent a lot more than that in my addiction, and I walked out the door.

Twin Lakes Center Unique Attributes

▸ Transportation to and from TLC residential programs

▸ A wide variety of treatment options related to the medical and mental health problems associated with chemical dependency, including crisis intervention.

▸ Direct access to all services of Somerset Hospital

▸ Small residential populations

▸ Campus style setting

▸ Recreational Therapy with several outdoor activities

▸ Nutritional Services provided by Marriott Services

NEED TREATMENT???
TO MAKE A REFERRAL OR FOR MORE INFORMATION CALL US AT
1-800-452-0218

Established in 1983, Twin Lakes Center sits on 30 acres of land in rural Somerset County. This remote, but easily accessible location provides a quiet, relaxing and positive recovery environment.

The Main facility provides residential and outpatient services to both adults and adolescents. From this base of operations, TLC has expanded over the years to include eight outpatient locations in various parts of Western and Central Pennsylvania

Services Include
Detoxification
Adult Residential
Adolescent Residential
Partial Treatment
Adolescent Re-entry
Intensive Outpatient
Outpatient
Evaluations
DUI Services
Prevention/Education

224 Twin Lakes Rd.
Somerset, PA 15501
Phone: 814-443-3639
Fax: 814-443-2737
24 hour ACCESSLINE
1-800-452-0218

TWIN LAKES CENTER
FOR DRUG & ALCOHOL REHABILITATION

ADOLESCENT UNIT

We can help you get your life back!

224 Twin Lakes Road
Somerset, PA 15501

24 Hour Accessline
1-800-452-0218

TWIN LAKES CENTER

Established Facility
Twin Lakes Center has been in operation for specialized Drug and Alcohol treatment since 1983, offering adolescent specific treatment for over a decade.

Experienced Staff
Twin Lakes Center staff is well versed in addressing the unique issues associated with adolescent substance abuse. Diverse backgrounds including Drug and Alcohol, Mental Health and Education— bringing over 35 years of combined experience.

Diversity
Various levels of care are available to adolescents age 13-18:

● Detoxification
● Short term residential treatment
● Day Treatment
● Outpatient
● All services of Somerset Hospital including behavioral health.

Individuality is The Key
The small size of the adolescent unit is its appealing feature, conducive to individual attention and personal growth. The 12 bed capacity encourages a "tight knit" community and a healthy "family like" environment. Small numbers allows for an excellent staff/adolescent ratio and individualized treatment. There will be no "getting lost in the crowd" allowed!

Family Involvement
Each weekend Twin Lakes Center staff conducts a family wellness program in order to get families involved and to understand the treatment and recovery environment of those working toward sobriety, as well as the disease of addiction. Again, the small size of this group allows for much personal intervention with staff and families. Family sessions are provided as part of both treatment and aftercare planning.

Recovery
The program is based on the disease model of chemical dependency utilizing the 12 step recovery program with the goal of ongoing abstinence and improvement in the quality of life for each person.

Structured Schedule
Each day is structured to include activities such as:

● Individual Counseling
● Group Counseling
● Lectures
● Recreational Activities
● 12 step meetings
● Personal Time
● Education needs met by certified professionals and coordinated with home school districts.

Admission Criteria
● Adolescents, male & female, age 13-18
● Meets Criteria for chemical abuse and/or dependency.

TWIN LAKES CENTER

(814) 443-3639
Access Line
1-800-452-0218

for drug and alcohol rehabilitation

P. O. Box 909 • Somerset, PA 15501-0909

Robert Anderson
2338 Franklin St.
Johnstown, PA 15905

October 30, 2007

Dear Bob,

This letter is to show appreciation for your years of service to the adolescent patients of Twin Lakes Center. For the past five years, your willingness to volunteer your time to chair NA meetings for the adolescent patients has made a difference in the lives of each adolescent in this program. The adolescents here are going through a very difficult period in their lives, and most of them have very little support upon completion of treatment. Your presence in their lives while they are in treatment and the knowledge you instill in them about the NA program and the support network it provides is a crucial part of the treatment they receive here. Twin Lakes appreciates the time and effort you give so unselfishly to all of the adolescents in treatment here, and we look forward to continuing your involvement in our program. Thank you!

Sincerely,

Breiann Howsare, LSW
Director of Residential Services

These are just a few of my many "Thank You" cards. They are my most prized possessions.

Bob,

Thank you very much for talking wit us. I learned many things, and could relate to it. When you were talking it gave me hope and I know I am not an addict now but if I keep going I will be. Thank You Again.

Alicia

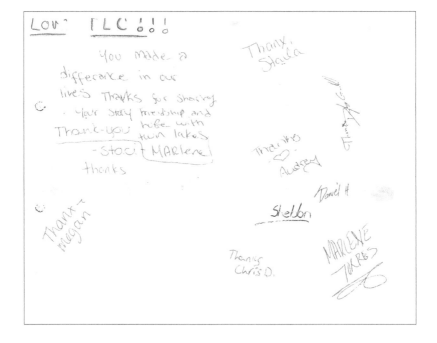

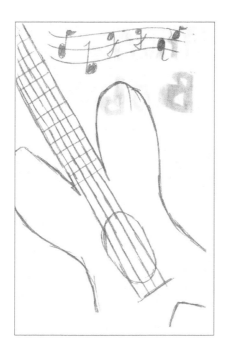

CHAPTER 52

DEJA VU

As I walked out of the church in Ebensburg, with a big box of supplies, I looked across the street, and a strange feeling of déjà vu came over me. I was looking at the front door of the old Cambria County prison, The "Stone Hotel". I had been a guest of the governor there eight years before. When they released me after 13 days and 14 nights in that hell hole, I remember being on those steps, looking this way! Everything in my life was the exact opposite of what it used to be. And out of 1 million buildings, what are the odds of these two buildings with their front doors facing each other?

Step two of AA says, We came to believe that a power greater than ourselves could restore us to sanity. Believe me, I was coming to believe!

At the adolescent meeting, the biggest concern of the kids was gaining their parents trust back. A lot of them had stolen TVs, stereos, etc. for drugs. I attended another meeting for parents of addicted kids. When I talked about the kids wanting their parent's trust back, one woman said something that stuck with me. She said, "I don't care about my stereo, I want my child back". I would tell the kids what this mother told me.

Some of the kids achieved long-term recovery. They would arrive at the rehab with dark, sunken eyes, never smiling or laughing, shaking uncontrollably, pale and sick looking. After 30 days, they would be healthy, smiling, and laughing, as I was. I would tell them, "This is just the beginning of your mind, body, and spirit healing". I would stress the importance of not picking up the first one. Don't give up before the miracle happens. The miracle is when the obsession goes away. A lot of kids were addicted to opiates, usually pills, but some had progressed to the needle. They had a wide range of drugs of choice. Everything from Coricidin, which contains dextromethorphan, to computer duster spray, inhalants, even gasoline as an inhalant. A lot of these caused immediate and permanent brain damage. I tried to educate these kids about the damage related to each drug. I also stressed the dangers of mixing drugs. I taught them about the high rate of overdose deaths, especially after a period of being clean. I loved all these kids, and they knew I cared about their well-being. They gravitated to me, and I got the feeling that they just needed to be loved and listened to. I wanted to bring them all home. A few of them died, and it was very hard on me. I told them addiction leads only to jails, institutions, and death.

Then I told them, "You're in an institution right now." I would bring my book bag, at least once a month. When I first got out of rehab, and I was cleaning my apartment, I put all the drunk in public papers, fine receipts, hospital papers, etc. into a book bag so I could look through it if I ever wanted to use or drink. This was a full-size bag, and it was completely stuffed with consequences. I would pull out stacks of consequences and stack it up on the table at the adolescent's meetings. Then I would put two speeding tickets next to that. I would tell them, "This stack is from addiction, and these two tickets are my only consequences for my years of recovery. Then I would show them the good things that happened to me in recovery. Nothing good ever happened in addiction. I would drive my hot rods to Somerset, and they would be inspired to stay clean. At some meetings, I would raise the topic, "What are your dreams?" After they all talked about what they wanted to do with their lives, I would say "Your dreams won't happen in addiction". A boy there once said, "I used to be in dirt bike competitions, and I was a first-place finisher. Now I have no desire to ride anymore, and I sold my dirt bike for drugs." I told him he could regain his dreams if he stayed clean and sober.

There were a few wilder kids now and then. They reminded me of myself. Once, a couple guys escaped to a local church, and stole the church van, to get back to their hometown. The kids ranged from 12 years old to 17. The meetings were very emotionally powerful. Sometimes there would be adults observing and taking notes. This would make the kids uncomfortable. At the end of every meeting, we would join in a circle, and say the serenity prayer.

I did the kids NA meeting for six years. Then they closed the unit. Instead of an adolescent and an adult unit, it was now a men's unit, and a women's unit. Over the six years, I estimate that I made friends with over 500 kids. In later years, I would see them everywhere, even in faraway towns in my travels.

CHAPTER 53

DYSFUNCTION

A t the Johnstown meetings, there was a lot of dysfunction, especially at the meetings in the center of town. They became a mixture of the men's and women's halfway houses. To add to the drama, the department of corrections guys would attend. A lot of the guys and girls acted like they were playing the dating game. The only requirement for membership in AA or NA is the desire to stop drinking or using. Most of these people had no desire to stop and didn't really belong there. The meetings were like their escape time from their facilities. The women would get all dolled up, and the men would act all tough. I talked to one woman who got pregnant in the parking garage, and she was proud of that. It made me sick! I thought to myself, that kid will never know his father. My friend Jackie had been singing on the microphone at my house, and talked about how much fun it was during the meeting. After the meeting, a guy from the DOC (Dept of Corrections) house told her he knew a producer from death row records. She fell for it and invited him to her apartment. Then he raped her. I took her to Pittsburgh for emergency contraception. She did not press charges like she should have. I saw this guy at a later meeting and confronted him about it. He just laughed at me, and said something like, "I'm all gangsta". I wanted to punch him in the face! Another time there was a DOC inmate at the welfare office, trying to recruit some of the girls to be prostitutes. I would call the supervisor at the DOC but they wouldn't do anything.

My recovery was now on solid ground. In early recovery, they say to stay focused on yourself. In later recovery, they recommend helping others. The newcomer is the most important person at the meeting. I would try to help the most at-risk people. I compare it to a sinking ship. I would try and help the women and the children first. To be completely honest, I was looking for a girlfriend, but I wouldn't want to derail anyone's recovery. There were a few women who were secure in their recovery. But none of them wanted a guy like me. If what doesn't kill you makes you stronger, I was the real tough guy, but I didn't brag about it. It seems so sad that the women fell for these fake guys.

I was completely misunderstood by most people. I hung out mostly with women and young people. The women knew I was a safe person, and the guys were jealous that they hung out with me. Maybe growing up with two sisters played a role too. I felt more comfortable around women. Most of the men seemed like they had a fake macho attitude. I stuck to the good people in the program. The meetings outside of downtown were always much better. People were there because they wanted to be there. Not because they had to be there. I saw at least 20 of my close friends die and I knew recovery was serious business. There is a fine line between helping people and enabling them. I would help them to help themselves. My friend Jackie, who I had taken to Pittsburgh, and her twin brother, Josh, would die from addiction. Jackie's aunt, Sarah, would be a casualty too. There were flowers at her viewing from Johnny and June Carter Cash. They were friends of the family. I had times where I felt like I was in a war zone, watching my friends die. I had to remove myself periodically, because it took such a toll on my happiness.

CHAPTER 54

JEFF

I rented a garage on the edge of Johnstown, where I fixed cars. One day I was under a car, and I heard someone say, "Is Bob Anderson here?" I looked out from under the car, and saw two nice looking dress shoes. At first, I thought they had finally caught up to me. As I climbed out, I saw it was my first counselor, Jeff. We had a few laughs, and he said it was good to see me, still clean, and sober. We became good friends and went to several concerts at the Palace Theater, in Greensburg, Pennsylvania. I fixed up an 86 Cadillac for him, putting another engine in it. It was a big white caddy with a red interior. He started the whole "New Visions" program at the hospital, and then started another company called "Independent family services". He had lots of counselors, working to keep dysfunctional families together. He had drug and alcohol outpatient programs, and other programs. I always enjoyed talking to Jeff. He had a wealth of knowledge, and I loved learning new things about psychology, counseling, etc. The walls of the office were wallpapered with degrees, diplomas, etc.

CHAPTER 55

INDEPENDENT
FAMILY SERVICES

I ended up volunteering at Jeff's drug and alcohol program. I must say, it was a lot more professional than Twin Lakes. I was required to pass several background checks, and be fingerprinted, even as a volunteer. Jeff sent me to some free training sessions, and I was working towards a certified recovery specialist certificate. I sat in on some groups, and shared my experience, and the things that had worked for me. At the Christmas party that year, I was awarded a plaque for my efforts.

There was another volunteer named Scott , who had a couple of years clean and sober. He relapsed on fentanyl, and was clinging to life for about a week before he passed. There was a prayer vigil for him behind the hospital. Everyone at IFS was devastated. We had all known him very well. We had a small meeting of just the counselors, and I talked a little about how emotionally draining this line of work could be. I talked about some of the kids who had passed away. We shared some happy stories of Scott too. He was quite a character.

These are my piles
of consequences from
addiction / alcoholism
(both piles)

The small stack of two
yellow speeding tickets were
my only consequences in
8 years of recovery.
I would show these to
the kids in rehab to
prove that 99% of my
problems came from addiction/
alcoholism.

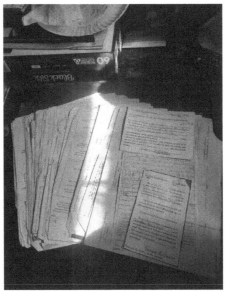

My second stack of consequences, 31 drunk in public arrests,
2 escapes, drug possession charges, etc.

CHAPTER 56

DR. ACOSTA

I was a temporary sponsor for a boyfriend and girlfriend in NA. Their names were Jim and Sarah. I let them use my car one day to run some errands. Afterwards, I found two papers on the backseat floor. They were medical papers from Dr. Acosta in Johnstown. Both papers were a long list of procedures, that were never done. The lists were identical for the both of them. He was defrauding Medicare, while dishing out large quantities of opiates. He was the biggest drug dealer around, and wore a white coat. He ended up fleeing the country, but he was eventually caught. I don't think he was dealt with as seriously as he should've been. At that time, I believe the opiate crisis had taken 400,000 lives. It's much higher now, especially with the arrival of fentanyl. I confronted Jim and Sarah about lying to me, and fired them as sponsees.

Meanwhile, Conemaugh hospital closed the detox unit. I guess it wasn't making them enough money. They also closed the New Visions program. This ticked me off to no end, because they would ask for people to buy a paper heart for one dollar, to fight the drug epidemic. Without a detox unit, I wonder if I would still be alive.

When I would help someone that needed to detox, I would take them to the emergency room, and they would have to say they were suicidal. This would get them into the mental health ward for a few days. If mental health doctors call it a mental illness, and addiction specialists call it a brain disease, then what the hell is the difference?

In my opinion, these two fields of medicine should be combined. 60% of addicts have co-occurring mental health issues. The system is broken. I suggested to a state representative three things that would make a difference.

1. Reopen the detox (it had a long history , going back to the founders of AA)
2. Make doctors and pharmacies accountable for the flood of opiates.
3. Educate children about the dangers of drugs and alcohol.

There's a lot more that could be done, like funding, treatment, etc. I also don't believe in methadone treatment. One of my friends calls it "diet heroin." I don't think opiate addiction can be treated with another opiate. Besides, the person is still dependent on a drug, not free.

CHAPTER 57

SLIPPING INTO DEPRESSION

At about 6 to 7 years, clean and sober, I felt unmotivated, tired, and depressed. I had just finished restoring a 72 Camaro, but I had a little interest in cruising around in it. That's when I knew something was wrong. In months before that, I would drive it through town, and it would really turn some heads. I even had an urge to stop into the bars that I used to hang out at. I was going to buy a round for everyone, and they would see me driving a cool car. When I first got sober, one of my main motivators was to show people what I was made of. They had ridiculed me many times. I would show them.

As I cruised past the bars, I realized I didn't have to prove anything to anybody. I stuck to my boundaries, and I didn't go in.

I consulted my counselor, Jeff, about my depression symptoms, and saw a doctor about it. There were non-narcotic medicines that could help me. They tried several until one particular antidepressant seemed to work. It also did a lot to help my social anxiety. I felt calmer.

Over the years, I have studied a lot about addiction, and the neurological aspect of it. One DVD that explains a lot is "Pleasure Unwoven." It is a ten-year study by a doctor, who struggled with his own addiction. The pleasure circuit of the brain is very complex. It's a wonder it can even heal itself. I believe I have done damage to my neurological system from drugs, alcohol, head, injuries, etc. One reason I wrote this book is in case I forget my past.

I witnessed the state of Anhedonia in the kids many times. That's when the pleasure circuit of the brain is basically dead, and only the drug can make the addict happy for a short time. The brain develops a tolerance for a large release of dopamine that is caused by the drug. Even a gambler who hits a jackpot will chase this high. The kids would say how badly they wanted a cigarette, and they were given Nicorette. When the kids arrived at rehab, they would not smile or laugh. When they left after 30 days, they would be smiling and laughing. I loved to watch them progress in their recovery. A lot of my adult friends did very well too. I even sponsored a heart surgeon for a while. I'm very careful to keep these names confidential.

Anyway, I found a happy medium with my depression. Too much medicine would make me tired, and too little would increase my anxiety and depression. I also did things that made me feel better, like playing guitar, walking, exercise, etc. I also discovered that I have seasonal depression, and I feel better when the sun is shining, and it's warm out. It's a never-ending process of improvements. My worst days are still 10 times better than my best days in active addiction. I will never be cured, and I must maintain my recovery.

CHAPTER 58

HOMEOWNER

In 2008, I was hanging out with my friend, Kelly, and her friend, Kathy. We were up on the mountain, at a junkyard that Kathy's family owned. She said, "Hey, let's take in some scrap metal for money, and we'll split the money". I filled up my pick-up truck, and we each got about 40 bucks. A couple days later, I got a car trailer, and we took in two cars for scrap. A day or two later, I got a call from the police. They asked me if I knew anything about a red Chevy Cavalier that was missing. I said, "Yeah, I took one in for scrap. I also took in a Dodge Caravan". The cop said, "What? You took two cars?" I said, "Yeah, the owner's niece, Kathy, said it was OK". The cop gave me the property owner's phone number, and I called him. I apologized for the confusion, and I offered to pay him back, and give him the receipt from the scrap yard. He agreed and I gave him 400 bucks. He said Kathy does this with any guy who has a pick-up truck. He was impressed by my honesty, and offered to sell me the property on a rent to own, article of agreement. I also talked him into no interest. He asked for $2,000 down, and $500 a month for three years. The total was $20,000.

On a visit to my aunt Sue, she gave me a 200-year-old violin, and I travelled to Philadelphia, to see Fred, a world renowned appraiser of stringed instruments. He was an appraiser for Christie's, antique road show, and more. He appraised it at $2500, and that's what I ended up getting for it. It covered the down payment, and the first month's rent, on my new property. When I first got the property, it was a mess, but I loved it! Kathy had let people dump couches, mattresses, etc. on the property. My brother-in-law, Pat, was married to Sandy. He was very helpful by lending me his big John Deere tractor, and he helped me with plumbing, electrical, carpet, and a new well pump, which was 300 feet below the ground. I took the tractor and pushed all the garbage into a big pile, and burned it. It reminded me of my recovery. First all the garbage had to go, to make room for the good stuff. There were two school buses, and a lot of cars. I got $2,000 for the two buses, and a lot more for the cars, and various scrap metal everywhere. The property was paying for itself! I stayed in a camper while I totally refurbished the house. I went from living in the woods, to owning 4 acres of it.

CHAPTER 59

LOSING TAMI

It was March 9, 2009. I was getting a truckload of coal for my heater. I had 12 years of recovery under my belt, without a relapse. I was dumping the coal, and I got very dizzy all the sudden. I collapsed to my knees, so I wouldn't fall. I wondered if I was having a stroke or something. I wondered how I was going to get help, since I was alone. After about a minute, it cleared up, and I went about my business. Later that day, my other sister, Sandy, called me and told me that Tami had committed suicide. She had shot herself in the head. I was completely overcome with grief, anger, denial, sorrow, and all the mixed emotions that go with losing someone so close. I believe we were so spiritually connected, that I felt her pain. She had been sober for six months, and was in touch with me a lot more than she was when she was drinking. I guess she got complacent and went back to bartending, and her husband who drank. She had relapsed. I called on my support group to help me cope, even though I didn't want to talk to anybody. Apparently, Tami had called my dad in Kansas to help her, but he wasn't any help. She was in San Diego, California.

A few months later, I finally got a chance to visit San Diego again. I had two nieces, Tami's daughters, that I had never met. They were now in their 20's, and I was excited to meet them. Their names were Erin and Jenny. They were both beautiful girls, and they were mourning too. I packed my Toyota Corolla (the C-Rolla), and grabbed my little dog, Tucco. I took out the front passenger seat and the backseat, to make a bed to sleep on. I saved a fortune on hotel rooms. I headed cross country, taking showers at the truck stops for 10 bucks, or at the YMCA for free. For some reason, hundreds of miles on the highway is very therapeutic for me. It was nice to get out of Johnstown for a while too. It took about a week to get there, and I watched the Saints win the Super Bowl, at a truck stop TV room. I arrived in San Diego and found a nice little park to hang out at, and take a nap in my car. This was before GPS, and I called my niece, to direct me where to go. She was amazed to find out that I was at the very park where Tami liked to hang out. She lived on the outskirts of the park, another amazing coincidence? I didn't believe in coincidences anymore.

I slept on Jenny's couch that night, and the next day I had dinner at a restaurant, with Erin and Jenny. We took some pictures with my disposable camera, and had a great time. We talked about Tami while we had dinner. Jenny had tried to help Tami so many times, and Erin had given Tami the "tough love" approach. I told them they were both right, and that they shouldn't feel responsible. I did my best to explain the insanity of addiction to them, hoping it would help them cope a little. It was so heartwarming to finally meet Erin and Jenny. They are such great girls!

The next day, I met Tami's husband, Butch. He was drinking a beer and told me Tami had taken the gun that he kept on the shelf by the TV, and gone out back into the shed, where she shot herself. He had her cremated after she died. While I was in California, I also planned to visit my mother's grave.

CHAPTER 60

VISITING MOM'S GRAVE

My sister Sandy had done some research on our family history, and we finally learned the truth about our mom's death. Sandy had uncovered autopsy papers that showed my mom died of a gunshot wound to the head, inflicted by her boyfriend, who then shot himself. Her blood alcohol content was .029, and she was only 29. At least we weren't left wondering anymore. She was buried at a cemetery in San Jose, north of San Diego. I went north on route five, and eventually found it. The people in the office directed me to her gravesite. I parked the car, and sat there, looking at her gravestone. It was a beautiful sunny day, and I couldn't believe it was this nice in February. All the sudden, the whole sky darkened above me, and about 1000 birds landed in the trees above me. I took some pictures of the trees, but the birds don't really show up in the pictures. I sat there for quite a long time, thinking I hadn't been this close to my mom in over 50 years.

CHAPTER 61

MIDNIGHT RADIO

I headed through San Francisco, and back towards home, taking route 80 across the country. I passed through Salt Lake City, where I was born, and saw the no trespassing signs along the road, where they did the nuclear testing. As I was traveling through Wyoming, at about midnight, I turned on the radio. I hadn't even listened to it much on the whole trip. It started playing "Daniel, my brother", by Elton John. Then it played "Glory Days", by Bruce Springsteen. That was Tami's favorite concert. Then it played "Do you feel like I do", by Peter Frampton. Tami, Sandy, and I, wore out that eight track tape, when we drove from Fairfax to Kansas, to visit our grandparents on our dad's side. We never knew anybody on our mom's side of the family. Then the radio played "Going up to the Spirit in the sky", by Norman Greenbaum. Tami and I both loved that song. Then, I crested a hill, and the radio station faded away. "Was it even a radio station?" I asked myself. There were no commercials, etc., only music. I had goosebumps all over! In my mind, it was Tami, telling me that she's OK. Another coincidence? I don't think so. 3000 miles had done me a lot of good, but it was great to get home. I guess it was more like 6,000, round trip.

CHAPTER 62

OWL STRIKE

When gas hit three dollars a gallon, I decided a motorcycle would eventually pay for itself. I found a nice Honda shadow 700 cc street bike. I had ridden a lot of dirt bikes before, but the street bike was a new thing.

I was riding down Saint Clair Road from my house, and I was cruising at about 45 mph. All of a sudden, something hit me hard right in the face. It was everything I could do, not to wreck. I slammed on the brakes and stopped. I got off the bike and walked back to where a large bird was laying on the road. When I saw the pointy beak and the eyes, I knew it was an owl. My first thought was to pick him up off the road, maybe he's just knocked out. I put him in my saddle bag and headed home. All I could figure, was that maybe the whine of the Honda sounded like an animal in distress to the owl. I wasn't hurt, but the next day I bought a helmet with a full-face shield. I called around to get this owl stuffed, as a memento of my first day of riding. They wouldn't do it, saying it was an endangered species. My sister gave it a proper burial, saying it's a very spiritual bird. I was now a hard-core biker. I killed an owl with my face!

CHAPTER 63

SHOULDER SURGERY

My brother-in-law, Pat, and I would ride the trails behind my house on the weekends. My house is on the Laurel Mountain Ridge, and adjoins the state game lands. It's a trail rider's paradise, with unlimited miles of woods. He was a motocross champion in Michigan where he grew up. He could ride a wheelie at 50 miles an hour and throw mud in my face with his back tire. I was riding a quad, and I would hit a big puddle to get him back. We had a blast! Once it started raining, but we were already so soaked in muddy water that it didn't matter. The rain was just rinsing off the mud. We were completely saturated.

I was climbing some big rocks and my quad tipped over. I reached out my arm to soften the landing, and I tore my rotator cuff in my shoulder. We headed back to my house, and I was riding with one arm. I knew it was serious because I couldn't raise my arm. It was my right shoulder and I'm right-handed. For my insurance to cover it, I was required to fail physical therapy. This was torture with a torn rotator cuff.

Eventually, I got the MRI done, and the doctor confirmed that I needed surgery. I wish they would've started with the MRI, instead of therapy. Anyway, on the day of the surgery, I told them I am a recovering addict, and I don't want any opioids or narcotics. The doctor kind of laughed, and said, this is going to hurt so bad, we're going to have a shot waiting for you when you wake up. I had to bite the bullet, and hope for the best. When I woke up, I had four holes in my shoulder, where they went in with cameras and everything else. They showed me pictures of the torn muscles. Before they would release me to my sister's care, I had to urinate for them. When I couldn't, they used a catheter on me. What a torture fest! I finally got out of there with my arm in a sling, and slightly elevated. I had holes going in the front and back and the sides of my shoulder. It hurt like hell! They prescribed me Percocet, one every four hours. I stuck to the instructions, even though I wanted to take twice that much. I would take one at 4, one at 8, and one at 12. They didn't make me feel high, since I took them as prescribed. I learned that they make a great painkiller when you take them the right way. The real trick was when the pain became bearable, and it was time to throw them away.

I learned that the only time opiates are appropriate is post operative pain. I would tell recovering addicts the two requirements. One, as needed, and two, as prescribed. Many addicts faced surgeries, and asked my advice. My friend Kelsee was very helpful, supporting me during my surgery. She took me to the grocery store, etc. I went to a couple AA meetings, and asked for help with my firewood, since I only had my left hand. Nobody helped me. Some of these people were all talk and no action. I had helped people move, I had given them furniture, etc. but when I needed a hand, they let me down. Oh well, I just kept on going. I started doing more for myself, and less for others. They would pay a fortune to get their car fixed at the shop, and they'd be mad at me. Oh well, I guess I wasted a lot of time fixing their cars the first 10 times I did it. When I examined my role in this, I realized that I had a pattern of "people pleasing".

I spent my 56th birthday in physical therapy, as my shoulder healed. I was born 12/12/56, and on 12/12/12, I turned 56. My only present was a T-shirt from the physical therapy office. What better way to spend my birthday, then a two-hour torture session?

I studied the NA book to determine if my surgery constituted a relapse. It has a lot to do with why the addict takes the drug. Did I take it to get high? No. Did I take it to kill pain? Yes. Did I discontinue use when the pain was manageable? Yes. This was not a relapse. It meant the difference between 13 years clean, or 13 hours. There was a mild withdrawal, after three days of Percocet as prescribed. My shoulder healed up good as new. I could even throw a baseball. The doctor wasn't sure if I would be able to. My shoulder looks like I was in a gun fight at the OK corral.

I was making great progress. I was facing problems, instead of running from them. I was resolving issues, instead of letting them pile up. My social anxiety was way better than it was. I used to walk into a room and wonder if the people would like me. Now I walk into a room and wonder if I'll like them. I was distancing myself from toxic people. My friends list got smaller and smaller. I realized a lot of these people were never friends to begin with. Even my sponsor drifted away when I stopped fixing cars for everybody. I had fixed his car many times. He had also done a lot for me though.

CHAPTER 64

TRIPS TO KANSAS

My dad's health was going downhill, and I drove to Kansas to visit him. I sorted out a lot of boxes and took a lot to Goodwill. He had been living alone, since Ida, our stepmother, had passed away from cancer. She smoked cigarettes, and I guess they caught up with her. On a previous trip, when Ida was alive, Sandy and I saw her mental health had gotten even worse. She cussed at everyone except me. I don't know why she hated everyone except me. She would sit at a little table in the middle of the kitchen that she had constructed from a chair, and sat in another chair. She would talk to imaginary people, and my dad would just say "Don't mind her." I went to the grocery store with her, and everyone stared. She was yelling at the clerk of the meat department about something stupid. Her hair was a mess, and she looked like the wicked witch of the west. On that trip, Sandy and I were riding into Topeka and a huge hawk, or something, was flying along next to us. Sandy and I both stared in amazement, as it flew 10 feet in front of our car for quite a while. I told Sandy, "I think Tami's spirit is with us" and Sandy agreed. It was an amazing sight!

Anyway, I made several trips to Kansas after Ida passed, and my dad was in the hospital from a fall. He made me executor of his will, and I had power of attorney. The will was made out to me and Sandy, so I made arrangements to fly her in for the paperwork.

CHAPTER 65

STEAK DINNER

Sandy and I were taking care of my dad's affairs in Kansas, while I still had power of attorney. If he was to pass away, I would lose power of attorney. There was a bank named Kaw Valley Bank, where Ida kept her money. Dad told me he was so proud of Ida for saving grocery money all these years. I wanted to tell him that she basically starved us, while he was working out of town all week. I would eat generic peanut butter and jelly. She would buy a huge box of powdered milk, and mix it up with faucet water. Then she would pour it into plastic gallon jugs, that she marked with lines. We were only allowed to drink the milk down to the next line each day. When dad was home on the weekends, she would make a big pot of spaghetti.

Anyway, I emptied the account which had $22,000 in it. Sandy and I each got a cashiers check for $11,000. I told Sandy "Hey, let's go get a steak dinner on Ida."

CHAPTER 66

DAD PASSES AWAY

I must have traveled to Kansas 4 or 5 times, to help my dad. He was still drinking his Budweiser at 92 years old. He would get dehydrated and fall. After a stay in the hospital, physical therapy, etc. I finally was able to bring him home to his assisted living. The first thing he did was dehydrate himself again, and got dizzy. I had to take him back to the hospital. My sister and I moved him to higher and higher levels of care. We weren't happy with the care he was getting, and moved him to a much smaller, better home. We were very unhappy with his first retirement community, so I won't mention their name. I was also very unhappy with the law firm that handled his estate. My dad's college friend was his lawyer there, but he had passed away. They charged me $80 for a one-hour visit, where they told me they had lost the paperwork.

Then they sent another bill for $80, totaling $160. I sent them a written letter, and never paid a cent. One of the last times I talked to my dad, was about Tami, and I'm not even sure if he felt bad about not helping her. I was trying to explain to him how alcohol is a depressant, and I had been in the same situation as Tami. There were a few times that I felt suicidal, and I sold the guns to be safe. He replied, "You sold that Winchester, that your grandfather gave you? That was worth at least $600!" I took that to mean that my life wasn't worth $600, and then I realized that in his drill sergeant mind, he doesn't understand. I guess I had insulted his precious alcohol too. He probably thought of Tami and I as wimps, and that we couldn't handle our alcohol.

While I was in Topeka, I visited the Evel Knievel Museum, which was really cool, and I went to a lot of AA and NA meetings there. I met a lot of good people there.

Eventually, my dad slipped away into dementia, and passed away. We were never very close, but it kind of hit me hard. I remember the good times and forgave the bad times. As I wrote earlier in this book, he didn't punish me when I threw the rock over the Catholic school. The rock didn't make it and broke a classroom window. All my friends ran away, but I stayed and fessed up to my mistake. The nun scolded me severely, and I thought I was in big trouble. When my dad got home, he bought me a brand-new baseball glove for telling the truth and standing up to what I did.

At his viewing, I slipped my baseball glove in beside him in his coffin. We had a beautiful ceremony for him in Topeka and he was buried next to Ida. He lived to be 92. My mom lived to be 29. We never knew anyone on our mom's side of the family. Now, it was just me and Sandy left in our whole family. We drove back from Kansas for the last time.

CHAPTER 67

BACK TO THE MOUNTAIN

Back at my home again, I built a garage to work on cars in. It has always been my dream to have my own garage, and restore classic cars. I have it all set up with a stereo system, and cable TV. I'm finally living my dream, but I have the aches and pains of my past to deal with. My property was paid off in 2013. I am living in peace and serenity up here, on top of the mountain. The air is fresh, and it's nothing but woods. I have my dog, Rocky, to keep me company. I can't seem to find an honest, sober, woman. And if I did, it would be hard for me to give up my freedom. She would have to be very special.

I can jump ahead to 2023, and I have no stories of bad things that happened. I've learned how to live the right way. I guess I had to learn the hard way.

To anyone struggling with alcoholism and addiction, there is hope!

As I finish writing this book, it's 2023, and I'm 27 years clean and sober!

Thank you Lord!

CHAPTER 68

FENTANYL WARNING

Today's addict faces a real danger of fentanyl, xylazine, and other synthetic additives, which have proven to be very deadly. In 2023, the overdose death rate was over 112,000. Today's drugs are an unpredictable mix of illegally manufactured fentanyl's, or IMF's, methamphetamines, and other new chemicals. The latest threats include the horse tranquilizer xylazine, which causes lingering flesh wounds, and nitazenes, synthetic opioids more powerful than fentanyl, Mexican drug cartels often press these chemicals into pills, which are made to resemble real medications for pain, depression, or ADHD. More Americans have died from fentanyl than from the Iraq, Afghanistan, and Vietnam wars combined. A dose as small as 2 milligrams can be lethal.

My good friend, Scott, overdosed on fentanyl, and passed away, after hanging on to life for a week in the hospital. He volunteered at the same facility that I did, until he relapsed and fell victim to fentanyl. Our whole drug and alcohol facility was in mourning, not to mention his family and all his friends.

The drug dealers don't care about you. The average drug has been cut about ten times, with God only knows what. Everything from baking soda, laxatives, drywall dust, soap powder, etc.

Let's educate our children, stop stigmatizing addiction, promote treatment, and hold pharmaceutical companies responsible. Addicts today are playing a deadly game of Russian roulette. In the words of Clint Eastwood, "Dyin ain't much of a livin."

Don't be a statistic. The best high is the natural high. You have a lot of living to do.

EPILOGUE

I wrote this book over two years, when the Covid pandemic was ravaging the whole world.

I once asked my counselor and friend, Jeff, why I had to go through so much suffering. He responded by saying, "If you hadn't, you wouldn't have such a story to tell the kids in rehab".

I guess he has a point.

I discovered that 99% of my problems came from drugs and alcohol.

The main reason I wrote this book, was to help the still suffering addicts and alcoholics in the world today. It's never too late to start all over again. (a great song by the 60s band Steppenwolf).

The first part of the book has so many bad stories of suffering, that I hope I didn't lose the reader. I actually left out most of the bad things that happened to me, so I would have enough paper. My stack of consequences is about 6 inches high. That would make a very fat book! My journey through hell as an addict/alcoholic was about 5 times as bad as I've described here.

WE don't have to live that way!

Notice how I emphasized WE?

DEDICATIONS

1. My sister Sandy
2. Jeff—counselor and friend
3. Mark—counselor and friend
4. Michelle—counselor and friend
5. Mike and Gail from Cedar Manor
6. Tammy—my caseworker
7. Kelsee, and her daughter, Delanee, who cheered me up with cuteness alone.
8. Pat—my brother-in-law
9. Casey
10. Jenny Anderson—transcriber and my niece
11. Erin Anderson—my niece

To all the family and friends I have lost

To all those suffering from alcoholism and addiction

Bob,

I remember calling you Motorcycle Bob for the longest time because thats how I knew you, coming to the Somerset meetings on your Harley ☺ Now when I mention you, I call you My Bob and everyone knows exactly who I'm talking about because they know how much I look up to you and pretty much recite every word you say because I can ALWAYS relate! Your strength in this program AND in real life is truly inspiring. When I start feeling bad for myself, I just play the tape of your story (at least what I know of it) through my head and it reminds me that no matter how bad it gets, TODAY there's nothing that can MAKE me pick up ☺ Thank you for that! I'm sorry that your card isnt as beautiful as the one that you gave me, I'm not as talented & artsy as you, but I try! Haha. This gift card is for you to go get some supplies and make something for yourself, like I'm sure you already thought of doing ☺ I know you to well, but you start on a little project for you! Remember Bob, this is your WORLD, we just live in it, haha. But seriously, thank you for my Sobriety♡ I hope you have an AMAZING BIRTHDAY!

I love you Bob,

Kelsee

225

ABOUT THE AUTHOR

Bob Anderson, born with birth defects from nuclear testing fallout, battled addiction, sharing his harrowing journey to 27 years of sobriety in *Victor*. A former auto-mechanic, Bob settled in Johnstown, PA, finding solace in classic cars, his dog Roxy, and playing guitar. His tumultuous life serves as a beacon of hope, inspiring those on the path to recovery.

Milton Keynes UK
Ingram Content Group UK Ltd.
UKHW020621220424
441543UK00007B/139